THE PARBOILED PASTOR

THE
PARBOILED PASTOR

The Joys and Pressures
of Parish Ministry

Steven L. McKinley

Augsburg
MINNEAPOLIS

THE PARBOILED PASTOR
The Joys and Pressures of Parish Ministry

Cover design by Mike Mihelich
Text design by James Satter

ISBN 0-8066-3633-5

The paper used in this publication meets the minimum requirements of American National Standard for Information Sciences—Permanence of Paper for Printed Library Materials, ANSI Z329.48-1984.

Manufactured in the U.S.A.   AF 9-3633

02   01   00   99   98   1   2   3   4   5   6   7   8   9   10

Contents

Preface

MANY BOOKS HAVE BEEN WRITTEN OVER THE YEARS BY WISE and insightful people concerning the theory and practice of parish ministry. Many of them are good and helpful books.

This is a book by a not-particularly-wise, ordinary pastor about the joys and sorrows, and the triumphs and tragedies, of being a pastor in a congregation. On the surface at least, it is not big on theory. It is big on reality.

My hope is simple. I hope that as you read through this book, as I lay my life open to you, you'll see yourself now and then. I hope that you'll feel a little less lonely out there on the mission field of ministry. I hope you'll be encouraged. I hope you'll even laugh now and then.

Since 1980, I've written a column called "Pastor Loci" for *Lutheran Partners* magazine, a journal for pastors and lay professionals of the Evangelical Lutheran Church in America. Since 1992, I've been writing another column, "The Parboiled Preacher," for *Academy Accents*, a publication of the Academy of Preachers. This book is a collection of some of the columns from both of those sources.

I've enjoyed the chance to do that writing over the years, in particular because of the feedback that has come my way from countless pastors who saw themselves in the various columns. I'm blessed with a great network of friends I've developed through the columns, many of whom I've never met, all of whom are sisters and brothers down deep, where it really counts. Whether or not we ever meet, I hope that when you've bounced around in this book a bit, you will also be one of those friends.

These columns, which appear as the chapters of this book, cover a period of eighteen years. Some show their age and reflect a time in my life different from today. While my life may be different now, I hope that the insights into the life of the parish pastor they reflect are still valid today. I think they are.

To God be the glory!

"How are you?" I asked a friend, and he said, "Grateful." A good answer.

Grateful. That's what I am as I share these columns with you.

Grateful to Ron Klug, the editor at Augsburg Fortress who winnowed his way through more columns than anyone should have to read to select the ones included in this book.

Grateful to Tracy Brownson, who faithfully and flawlessly prepared them for preparation, quietly doing her own polishing along the way.

Grateful to the people of Gloria Dei Lutheran Church, Forestville, Connecticut; Trinity Lutheran Church, New Haven, Connecticut; Bethel Lutheran Church, Auburn, Massachusetts; Christ the King Lutheran Church, Windsor, Connecticut; Grace Lutheran Church, Andover, Minnesota; and House of Prayer Lutheran Church, Richfield, Minnesota, the congregations of my life.

Grateful to K. Alvar Persson, Bob Endruschat, and Fred Auman, my first mentors in ministry.

Grateful to countless pastors who, over the past thirty years, have been partners and fellow workers, whose experiences and insights have shaped my own perceptions. We've shared laughter and tears and life, and it has been good.

Grateful to people like Carl Uehling, Bill Decker, and Carl Linder, whose editing of my work has converted more than one sow's ear into something approaching a silk purse. But my greatest gratitude goes finally in three directions.

First, to that great and whimsical God whose divine sense of humor is reflected in God's calling of me to the ministry.

Second, to Dick Koenig, the first person who believed I could write something that would be of interest and use to the church, the one who gave birth to "Pastor Loci." His editing saved me on many occasions. His encouragement kept me writing. His friendship kept me excited.

Finally, to our children, Jill, Kirk, and Meg; and to my wife, Pat, who was the first person to read virtually all of these columns, and who more than once set me on a better course than I would have followed left to my own devices. Their love has been and is for me "a foretaste of the feast to come."

Steven L. McKinley

THE WORK
OF THE MINISTRY

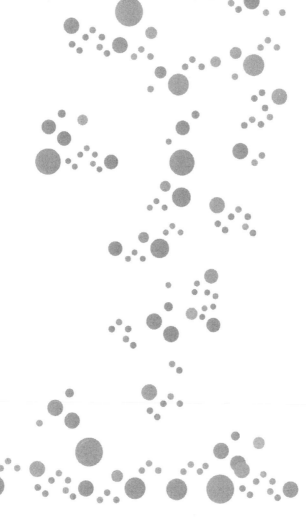

Why I Am (and Remain) a Parish Pastor

IT WAS, I SUPPOSE, A CLASS ASSIGNMENT. ANYWAY, THE YOUNG lady looked at me intently and asked, "Why are you a parish pastor?"

You would have been proud of me. I gave all the right answers we learned a long time ago. I talked of sensing a call of God, of finding my life directed in a certain way. I put in the good stuff about the priesthood of all believers, about pastors being set apart to perform a particular kind of ministry but not set above the laity. You know the speech as well as I do. Maybe better.

She seemed to take it seriously. At least she wrote it down, and that always inflates the old ego. But after she thanked me and went on her way, I thought about the question a little more, and I realized that while I had told her the truth, I had not told her the *whole* truth. To tell the whole truth forces me to say something that is at least unfashionable in clergy circles, and sometimes seems to border on heresy.

You see, my little secret is this: I am a parish pastor because it is fun to be a parish pastor. Fun seems to be a cheap little nontheological word to use for ministry, but I'll stand by it. My dictionary defines fun as "a source of enjoyment or pleasure," and that is exactly how I feel about the parish ministry.

Holding a baby during the baptism is fun. As the years go by, I find that I hold onto them longer and longer. They gurgle and cry and play with my pectoral cross. The parents get embarrassed, but I'm having fun.

Preaching is fun. The challenge of proclaiming the good news of God active in Jesus Christ turns me on. The adventure of relating the word of God to the struggles of everyday living gets my juices flowing. Sometimes it works and sometimes it doesn't, but getting there is half the fun.

Life-sharing is fun. As a pastor, I get to stand with people at life's most significant intersections: birth, baptism, marriage, sickness, unemployment, death. It is a unique privilege for me to be a part of all that. Some of the intersections themselves are anything but fun. But the chance to share life with others is fun.

Flexibility is fun. Sometimes I think that we as pastors overlook the opportunities we have to be flexible in our schedules. There is always work to be done, but there is not a clock to be punched. If my wife and I decide over lunch on a beautiful day that we would like to get in nine holes of golf that afternoon, the clubs are in the car in no time. If our children have a parent-teacher conference at school, I go sit in a little chair. If the grass desperately needs to be cut, I get out the old clothes. Of course, pastors cannot always be flexible; some things cannot be put off or shifted. But there is in the schedule of the parish pastor great opportunity for flexibility. And enjoying flexibility is fun.

Making a difference is fun. As parish pastors we make a difference in the life of a congregation and in the lives of individuals. Very few people can make a difference in the way a parish pastor can. Sometimes the difference we make is less apparent than real, but we do make a difference—for good or ill. And that is fun.

Then there are countless little "fun things": the pictures of the pastor drawn by the class of six-year-olds . . . the coffee and special cookies shared by that sweet little lady each time you visit . . . putting the "Clergy: Official Business" sign in the car window when you park overtime

. . . being ushered to the front of the line at the potluck supper . . . the annual flood of Christmas cards. They are little things. They are ego things. But they are fun.

Now let me reassure you that my parish is not in Disneyland. Some of the things I do are not fun at all. They are tedious and boring at the least, heartbreaking at the most. There's a lot of pain in the parish, and we share it and make it our pain. There is an inherent loneliness in the parish ministry.

But there is also in the ministry the potential for a great deal of fun. (If *fun* is still too frivolous a word for you, substitute *satisfaction*. But I prefer *fun*.) And the fact that I do have fun with what I do makes me more certain of the call of God. I've always liked what Frederick Buechner says about *vocation* in his book *Wishful Thinking: A Theological ABC* (New York: Harper and Row, 1973, p. 95):

> The kind of work God usually calls you to is the kind of work (a) that you need most to do and (b) that the world most needs to have done. If you really get a kick out of your work, you've presumably met requirement (a), but if your work is writing TV deodorant commercials, the chances are you've missed requirement (b). On the other hand, if your work is being a doctor in a leper colony, you've probably met requirement (b), but if most of the time you're bored and depressed by it, the chances are you have not only bypassed (a) but probably aren't helping your patients much either.

For me, the parish ministry meets both requirements. I am convinced that it is a work that the world needs to have done. I am also convinced by my own experience that it is a work I need to do. The fun I have "doing ministry" is what convinces me of that.

I write these words in the full awareness that some ministry situations lend themselves to "fun" more than others do. Certainly pressure and heartbreak and dullness and dark days appear in every ministry. Ministry is serious business. But deep within it there is also a deep font of plain, old-fashioned fun. As you carry out your ministry in your place, I hope that you never lose touch with your font of fun.

Why am I a parish pastor? In fact, there are two reasons: I am a parish pastor because I feel called by God to the parish ministry, and I am a parish pastor because it is fun.

Then again, maybe that's only one reason.

Dorothy's World

DOROTHY WAS PROPPED UP IN HER BED, FACING TOWARD THE window, when I came in the door. I was surprised that Cliff wasn't there. I knew he spent most of his time there with his wife of fifty-four years.

Dorothy had just entered this lovely nursing home a few weeks before. It was my first visit to her in her new surroundings. Her eyes were closed, and I stood there for a minute looking at her, all prim and neat, every hair in place, her makeup immaculate. I called her name. Her eyes popped open.

"Pastor, it's good to see you. How nice of you to come on such a busy day. Please sit down."

"Well, Dorothy, most days are pretty busy," I said, taking a chair next to her bed.

"Yes, but today must be especially busy. I know it is for me. I just have a few minutes to talk. I need to help my mother get dinner ready. But pastor, I want to tell you that I thought the services last night were just beautiful. The best ever. Christmas Eve is my favorite night of the year."

Now I knew for certain that we were in trouble. It was, you see, not Christmas Day, but a Friday afternoon in April, ten days before Easter. I had come to share Easter communion with Dorothy.

Mouthy fool that I am, I told Dorothy just that. She would have none of it. As far as she was concerned, it was Christmas Day. We were also not in a nursing home, but in her mother's house, in a part which she and Cliff were using as an apartment. Her mother was in the kitchen preparing Christmas dinner. In a really odd twist of things, my mother was there, too, helping Dorothy's mother in the kitchen.

In terms of what you can see and hear and taste and smell and touch and prove scientifically, Dorothy was far removed from reality. Not Christmas Day, but a Friday in April. Not her mother's house, but a nursing home. Her mother and my mother both long dead. But Dorothy was living in a subjective reality all her own that day. She was happy there.

I had a decision to make. I knew that the objective reality around us was far different from the subjective reality of Dorothy's world. I knew that it was April, that we were in a nursing home, that I had come for an Easter communion. I had to decide which world I was going to minister in—the "real world" or Dorothy's "world."

Here is what I did. I went to Dorothy's world.

We had communion all right. But rather than using the Easter scripture text I had marked in my Bible for the occasion, I turned over to Luke 2 and read the Christmas story. In response to Dorothy's request, we sang "Silent Night" together, though her voice was shaky and I always fall into the category of the singing impaired. And we talked, talked at length, of the glories of Christmas and Christmas trees and Christmas cookies and Christmas gifts and Christmas cards; of how much we both enjoyed Christmas and the memories we have of Christmas and how hard mothers work to make Christmas memorable. On a Friday afternoon in April. Had you been in my place (and I expect that some of you have been in that place), you would have done the same thing.

As you read this story—and as I write this story—it sounds absurd, ridiculous, maybe even humorous. Indeed, when I told my family of my visit with Dorothy over the dinner table that night, we laughed about it. But I must tell you that my visit with Dorothy that afternoon was a precious and tender moment, and a communion I will never forget.

As the senior pastor of a large congregation, I like to think of myself as a leader. As you know, "leadership" is a hot topic for clergy today. So as I sat in Dorothy's room, I kept thinking of that famous quote from Max Dupree: "The first responsibility of a leader is to define reality."

Most of the time I take that responsibility very seriously. I define reality for the congregation I lead. That has been and is a major part of my ministry at House of Prayer. I help the congregation recognize a reality which is significantly different from the reality that many of our folks remember in the heyday of this congregation thirty or forty years ago. I help them own up to the painful fact that next year will not be 1963. I have done that in the past, and will continue to do that in the future.

But on that particular day, in that particular nursing home room, with that particular Dorothy, it seemed right to abdicate the reality-defining throne, and immerse myself in the reality which is so vivid for Dorothy. In that tension we all live with of being servant leaders, it seemed best at that moment to stress that servant end of things, and allow Dorothy to be the one to define reality.

I do not tell you this story to publicly pat myself on the back for being an exemplary pastor. I do not think of myself as that. I'm not sure that what I did that afternoon was "the right thing" to do. I do not tell you this story to propose some new paradigm for pastoral ministry. The world is already packed with people who are into pioneering professional pastoral paradigm proposals. (Try reading that sentence out loud quickly a few times!)

No, I simply tell you this story because I think of you as friends, colleagues, and partners, and this was a rich and moving time for me I wanted to share with you. It was a small moment, but a great moment.

Communion was over, and we shared our Christmas memories. "Pastor, I have to get back to work now," Dorothy said. "My mother is counting on me. Thank you for coming today." Her arms reached up toward me, and we hugged.

"Merry Christmas, Pastor."

"Merry Christmas, Dorothy."

As I closed the door behind me, I looked back one last time to Dorothy, sitting there with a contented smile on her face, looking out the window, looking out at a world where she was young, and her mother was in the kitchen, and it was Christmas Day, and the services the night before had been beautiful . . . the best ever. I counted it a privilege to have shared that Christmas with her.

What Makes the Pastor Run?

I T WAS THE DAY BEFORE OUR SYNOD CONVENTION WAS SCHEDULED to begin. I was hip-deep in work while getting ready for the convention, making sure that everything was set for Sunday, etc. In the midst of that hubbub I got a telephone call from one of our active members. Tom reported to me that he had called Dick and Edith the night before about a project underway in the congregation. Edith had told him that they were not interested, since "we are transferring to another congregation in the area."

This was news to me, and certainly not good news. Dick and Edith were charter members of the congregation. Dick served on the call committee when I came here. He helped build our house. They had been stalwarts of the congregation since its birth. While they had not been in church every Sunday, I had certainly seen them and talked to them with some regularity. And now this.

As soon as I hung up the phone I dropped everything I was doing and headed for their house, only to learn that they had already gone away for the weekend. So I went off to the convention and spent most of my time stewing about Dick and Edith. I ran down the list of possible reasons they might have had for leaving. It did not take long for me to reach the chilling conclusion that they were leaving because of me.

I was able to complete a home visit with them the following Monday. I learned then that their decision to leave was based on a recent action of the church council to allow the youth of the church to have a dance in our parish hall, which was the original sanctuary of the church. At least, that was what was said to me, and to the president of the congregation when he called on them.

A few weeks later my day got off to a flying start with a hot debate about our denomination's position on abortion at the men's Bible study breakfast. Later in the morning I had a surprise visit from an old friend, then called on one of the true saints in the congregation who had just begun a new series of radiation treatments aimed at two new outbreaks of cancer in her body. I next had a lengthy lunch with one of our members, and spent a good deal of time talking with him about his marital problems. I returned to the church for a farewell party for our intern. He and I had a very close relationship, so this was not a particularly cheery occasion, and I was also acutely aware that I was fighting my worst cold in several years.

Just as the ice cream and cake were being served, Jim came in and asked if he could talk with me for a few minutes. We sat down in my study. "We're leaving Grace Lutheran Church," Jim said. "We aren't being spiritually fed here anymore. We just can't go along with the liberal, nonbiblical theology of the Lutheran church any longer."

Jim and Betty had been part of my Word and Witness class, and I knew that we were poles apart theologically. Nonetheless, I have a deep personal affection and respect for them. Jim assured me that the feeling was mutual, and that they appreciated what I was doing at Grace, but was adamant in his feeling that it was time for them to go to a church more in tune with their theological position. It was not an easy decision for them, Jim said, since they were also charter members of Grace Lutheran Church.

Two charter-member families of the church gone in the space of a month! Both active families. Both faithful stewards. Both respected in the congregation. Gone.

They said it wasn't me. But it is difficult for me to be convinced. I have a problem with coordination. In my head I know what they said, and I have no reason to think that they are not telling me the truth. In my head I know that these things happen. A few families will leave a parish roughly one year after a new pastor begins. I even recognize that this is sometimes for the best. In the case of Dick and Edith they have many friends and family members in their new congregation, and their new congregation offers more for people in their age bracket than does ours. Jim and Betty are closer to the Evangelical Free Church in their theology then they are to the Lutheran Church.

My head has all these things down perfectly. But my heart is not always in step with my head, and in my heart I feel a sense of failure. I can't shake the conviction that in making such decisions, people are finally questioning my fitness to be a pastor. In spite of what I say to myself, that then leads *me* to question *my* fitness for the ordained ministry. (Is there something in the nature of our calling that impels us to draw such conclusions? Or is it only me?)

I don't want you to worry about me, if you are so disposed. I have a loving and supportive wife, an excellent group of colleagues, a superior bishop, an adequate base of support in the congregation, and a rich reservoir of Scandinavian stubbornness, in addition to an abiding faith in the God who called me to this particular vocation and will supply me with the grace to survive.

But I hold up these painful experiences before you because I am confident that most of you have had (or will have) your own Dicks and Ediths, Jims and Bettys. They represent the deepest fear we all have as pastors, the fear that we are being judged by our people and that someplace, somewhere, sometime someone will find us wanting, which will then lead us to judge ourselves as wanting.

I wonder if it is not that fear—irrational though it may be—as much as it is our faith that keeps us as pastors knocking ourselves out to do the very best job we can in everything that we do. Though we don't like to say it out loud, such fear is a constant companion for many a parish pastor.

What makes the pastor run? Is it faith, or is it fear? I don't know about you, but for me I must confess it is both.

Words of Wisdom
for the "Singing Impaired"

I AM NOT A PERSON WHO HAS GREAT NEW CREATIVE IDEAS, BUT I do know a good idea when I see one. Our brother Bob Hock from Winter Park, Florida, was the chaplain at a church convention, and he made a powerful impression on that critical congregation. I found his final sermon particularly striking. It had to do with peace building. As he came to the end of the sermon, he said something like, "I'd like to close this sermon with a song on this theme that is very popular in our congregation. Feel free to join in if you know it." And immediately, in his rich baritone voice, he launched into "Let there be peace on earth, and let it begin with me." Marvelous. Impressive. Throughout the convention hall people were singing and daubing at their moist eyes.

As I dried my own eyes, I knew that I had seen a good idea. Now it was time to make it my own. When I returned home to Minnesota, the Land of 10,000 Johnsons, I began plotting the right time to spring it on my congregation. It would be sensational.

The Second Sunday in September, Rally Sunday, Kick-Off Sunday, Congregational Life Sunday. Like the swallows returning to Capistrano, Minnesota, Lutherans return to worship on the second Sunday in September, and the new program year begins. Time for a barn-burner sermon to rally the troops.

Well, I gave it to them good. I talked about God's manifold gifts to us. I talked about the mission challenges before us. I talked about worship, witness, learning, service, and support; about paying off the debt; about tithing; about loving one another; about the new Lutheran church and how it will enrich our ministry. And then I was ready with the heavy artillery. "All of this reminds me of one of my favorite songs. Feel free to join in if you know it." I put back my head, took the microphone in my hand, and started to croon. "To dream, the impossible dream, to fight the unbeatable foe . . ." Well, by the time I was bearing with the unbearable sorrow and running where the brave dare not go, two-thirds of the congregation was hustling toward the narthex, with my wife and children leading the way in abject humiliation. The congregation was rescued from synodical administration only by my solemn promise never to sing out loud in church again.

I am, you see, a member of that unsung minority, the singing impaired. While my singing sounds marvelous to me, others detect flaws in it. Frankly, I cannot even recognize when I am off-key and out-of-tune, which I usually am. On occasion I try to forget about my shortcoming and sing like any other pastor, but those who love me (and love music) are quick to point out my failings, and bring me back to earth.

It isn't easy being a singing-impaired pastor. It isn't easy in a church whose worship gurus suggest that God is offended when the liturgy is spoken. It isn't easy when conventions push for pastor's choruses. It isn't easy when you would like to introduce some new liturgy, or maybe a new hymn.

In spite of the embarrassment, some of us who are singing impaired are now coming out of the closet. Our esteemed Bishop Crumley commented in Toronto that one of the few direct words from the Lord he has received was, "Crumley, I didn't give you a singing voice, so don't."

We singing impaired are understanding people. We are not asking for proportionate representation in the legislative assemblies of the Lutheran church. We are not asking for someone to organize a telethon on our behalf.

All we ask for is a little understanding, the recognition that being singing impaired does not disqualify a person from ministry. Please understand that it is not that we don't want to sing. It's just that, for some reason, we can't do it, anymore than a person in a wheelchair can pole vault.

The ugly truth is that all of us have our handicaps. Some of us are singing impaired. Some of us are preaching impaired. Some of us are teaching impaired. Some of us are administration impaired. Some of us are visitation impaired . . . youth impaired . . . finance impaired.

The glorious truth is that we can be, and are, pastors just the same. Recent studies of what people expect from their pastors have made it clear that what people look for has more to do with character than skills, more to do with faith than ability. Our people will happily put up with all of our handicaps as long as they get the feeling that faith and love live in us. Ministry has more to do with *being* than *doing*.

This is not an excuse for laziness. There are helpful skills for ministry. We can and should improve our abilities to carry out the manifold duties which are part of the ordained ministry in the parish.

But we should be wary of identifying ministry only with a certain set of skills. In my case that means that I can be a pastor even though I am singing impaired, as long as some sense of faith, some sense of God active in Jesus Christ to bring the forgiveness of sins and the promise of eternal life, and some evidence of a personal relationship to God are at the core of my being.

That, perhaps, points us at the divine comedy that is the ministry. I knew a pastor once who was a terrible preacher—but a great pastor. Another thought she was too quiet to "make it" in the ministry, but proved to be a beloved rock to her congregation. Another fine pastor feels faint every time he enters a hospital room. But somehow, somehow, God takes all of us and makes us the ministers of the gospel. We pastors might be a handicapped lot. God deserves better than us. But we are the ones who have been called to ministry, in spite of our handicaps. Or maybe because of them.

That reminds me of a song. But I'm not going to sing it. I promise.

Let's Not Rely on Paper

B ECAUSE I WAS THE ONLY ONE IN THE OFFICE AT THE TIME, I took a phone call the other day from the good folks who sold us our photocopying machine five years ago. We keep a service contract with them, which is based on the number of copies we make in the course of a month. The caller wanted me to look inside the machine at the little dials that tell us how many copies we have made. She would then compare that number to last month's number, which would then tell us what the bill for the month would be. After I said the number, I sat back and thought about it.

In five years we have made nearly 750,000 copies. That's three-quarters of a million copies. Three-quarters of a million. I got out my paper and pencil and abacus and slide rule and went to work. We use a lot of legal-sized paper here for bulletins and so forth. Figure that half of the 750,000 went into legal-sized copies; half into regular sized. That totals up to nearly 150 miles of paper. Try to picture that in your mind. Think of the distance between your home and a favorite place 150 miles away. If you think in biblical terms, picture the distance between Jerusalem and Damascus. If you are a long-distance runner, picture six marathons—back-to-back. 150 miles.

The number stuck in my mind. I was so obsessed by it, in fact, that I began a research project to find out exactly how we "spent" those 150 miles. I am happy to report to you herewith the distribution of our 150 miles of copies.

The first 125 miles turned out to be pretty routine. Church bulletins. Newsletters. Annual reports. Minutes. Financial reports. We produce them just like you do. It occurs to me sometimes that our bulletins and newsletters and annual reports and minutes are probably interchangeable. You could send me a year's worth of yours, and I could send you a year's worth of mine, and all we would have to do is change a few names, dates, and addresses, and we would be ready to go.

If it were late December right now, for example, you would probably be producing the January church newsletter. I bet I know what would be in it. You would urge people to attend the annual congregational meeting. You would remind a few sluggards to pick up their offering envelopes from the tables in the narthex. You would thank people for their Christmas generosity. You would report that there are still a few Sundays available for donating flowers—see the flower chart or call the church office. Of course, you would list the circle meetings and the pre-Lenten study program and the youth ski trip/sledding party/sleigh ride (unless you happen to live in some warm part of the country). Our first 125 miles of paper would be remarkably similar to the paper which comes out of your church office.

We have now accounted for 125 of the 150 miles. But we're just getting to the good stuff. The last twenty-five are the most interesting miles:

1 mile of body parts

Yes, Junior, the copy machine will make a copy of your handprint. Your elbow. Your foot. Your ear. Other things, too, but since this is a church office, we do not copy those.

2 miles of Christmas pageants

Only the teachers care about the script. Everybody knows the best parts of the pageant aren't in the script—like when the toy doll that is assigned the role of the baby Jesus gets dropped and rolls down the chancel stairs, and Mary and Joseph get in a fight over who did the dropping and who will do the picking up.

10 miles of personal work

"I was just in the neighborhood and thought I'd stop by the church to pray. Oh, there is a copying machine here? I didn't know that. Do you suppose I could make up to fifteen or twenty copies of Aunt Verna's recipe for fruit-cake? Everybody loves Aunt Verna's fruitcake."

5 miles of pure waste

Trial runs. Paper the wrong size. Machine needs fluid. Repairperson testing the machine.

1 mile of music

Of course we know that it is strictly illegal to copy music on a copy machine, so we never do this. At least, not very often. Only when we really need it. Or it is too expensive for us to buy. Or it would take too long for it to get here.

3 miles of pictures from coloring books

Now and then Sunday school teachers get totally desperate.

3 miles of miscellaneous

Sermon copies. Memos. Lesson plans. Letters. Christmas letters. Cartoons. Diagrams of football plays. You name it, we got it.

Well, that's it. That's how we spent our 150 miles of paper. A lot of trees sacrificed their lives to keep this place going. In my cynical moments, I wonder what good it did.

You see, I am old-fashioned enough to be a great believer in the printed word. But I am not a fanatic about it. I hope that we do not put too much faith in the power of the paper we produce. Not many lives are changed by newsletters or church bulletins or financial reports or pastoral letters or annual reports or committee statements or convention studies. A few, maybe—but not many.

As we seek to communicate the great good news that has been entrusted to the church and build up the life of the family of faith, we will certainly continue to produce paper. But the most profound communication and the most productive upbuilding will come from flesh-and-blood sharing of people with people. Paper is much neater than people are. Paper is much less painful than people are. But people are what it is all about for us. When God sought to get God's message through to us, God did not dictate a pastoral letter and run if off on the heavenly photocopying machine. God sent Jesus Christ. There's a lesson in there somewhere. Let's continue to *use* paper, but let's not *rely* on paper.

Carl, Emma, Joan, and Jerry

CARL WEARS DARK SAFETY GLASSES ALL THE TIME. HE HAS a perpetual seven-day beard and gray hair that flies off in every direction. He never looks clean. He loves to corner me and tell me about the sins of other pastors. He rambles on about how the church of today is not like the church of his boyhood some sixty-odd years ago. Congregational meetings are not complete without a speech to that effect from Carl. When faced with opposition, he threatens violence. He seems to take particular pleasure in intimidating women.

Emma is his wife. She is sweet and meek and younger than Carl and sings in the choir. She seems in a perpetual daze and is always surprised when anyone remembers who she is.

Not long ago Carl and Emma were evicted from the furnished apartment they have shared since they were married after the two of them met at a local mental hospital. They did not have the financial resources to buy the furniture they needed for their new apartment. They threw themselves on our mercy. The congregation was able to help them.

The congregation could not have a more faithful choir member than Emma. When it snows, Carl takes charge of plowing the parking lot, as his gift to the congregation. They are productive members of the church. But they are, to use a gentle word, *eccentric*. Most people steer clear of them.

Joan is also eccentric. She is a widow in her fifties. Joan has spent a lifetime fighting with mental illness and alcoholism. For the moment she is winning the fight. She has not had a drink in several years. She keeps herself together and goes many places. But her emotions run close to the surface, and her conversation goes off in many different directions. Joan is doing her best as a mother and grandmother. She studies scripture faithfully, even if she does not always understand it. She overflows with good intentions. You never know what Joan is going to say. You never know when she will begin to cry. That makes people nervous. They do their best to avoid her. Joan is eccentric.

Jerry was the resident eccentric in my last congregation. A widower, he was doing his best to rear four teenagers. He had a history of epilepsy. Jerry held a good job as an engineer. He was one of the "biggest givers" in the congregation some years. But he rebelled at dressing up for church, saying that he had to dress up enough to go to work. When Jerry showed up for worship on Sunday morning, he clearly had not shaved or washed since Friday morning. He always wore an old, baggy gray sweater, a madras plaid shirt, nondescript pants, and elderly moccasins. He preferred to sit by himself in the front of the church. That was okay with everyone else. Jerry made people nervous. They did their best to avoid him. Jerry was eccentric.

When I was learning about ministry, nobody ever told me about the eccentrics. Oh, of course they told me about people with "problems." But they were always neat, conforming people, who would come into my office from time to time and cogently articulate the burdens on their hearts and souls. I would use all manner of good counseling technique, then send them back out into the world healed. No one's necktie would be messed in the whole process. It would be very neat, and clean, and sterile.

As is so often the case, reality did not live up to the vision. While most of my people in all of my congregations have been reserved, polite, and presentable, each congregation has also had its eccentrics. In terms of the nervous toll they take on a pastor, one eccentric is worth five "regulars."

What draws them to our congregations when they live in isolation from the rest of society? It is probably theological. After all, we say that God loves you as you are. Our eccentrics have the nerve to take us seriously.

Like any good preacher, I have told my congregation for years that we as Christians are called to love the unlovable. I have illustrated by talking about the imprisoned, the politically different, and so forth. But lately I have come to realize that the eccentrics often fall into the unlovable category, too. Carl is not an easy man to love, particularly when he is talking about separating the heads of church council members from their shoulders. But our exorbitant Christ had the gall to die for Carl and to label him "loved" in the process.

That, perhaps, is the greatest value of eccentrics to our congregations. They challenge us to live out the gospel we preach. Any congregation that does not have a few eccentrics (a situation I now find beyond the imagining) is missing out on something.

I might still groan inwardly when Carl corners me in the kitchen for one of his diatribes. I might want to hide under my desk when Joan drops in to share her latest big idea, or big heartbreak. But I would not want my church to be without them, not really.

If the bishop stops by, my eccentrics might be there to greet him. No need to be embarrassed. He will understand. After all, he probably thinks of *me* as one of his eccentrics.

Keep at It, Charlie Brown!

AREN'T YOU SICK OF SERMON ILLUSTRATIONS ABOUT "PEANUTS" cartoons? So am I. Charlie Brown is cute and Linus is deep, but enough is enough. Time for a moratorium on "Peanuts" illustrations.

But until some officially anointed executive declares the moratorium . . .

Good ol' Charlie Brown has a great attitude about baseball. For as many years as Charles Schulz has been grinding out cartoons, Charlie's team has been losing, and losing badly. Poor Charlie, as both captain and pitcher, he stands out on the mound and goes crazy as his team falls apart around him. Nevertheless, Charlie is a congenital optimist. Every time a new season rolls around, Charlie believes that this is going to be *the* season when his team wins a game, and maybe even the championship. Maybe this time his pitches will be true, his fielders alert, his hitters powerful.

Of course, it never works out that way. An inning or two into the first game of the season, Charlie will be out on the mound, dodging line drives and watching Lucy in right field pick daisies while fly balls drop all around her. And now Charlie knows. This will *not* be the year. He had all the right dreams, all the high ideals, but this year will be just like all the rest.

I approach confirmation teaching the same way Charlie Brown approaches baseball. My history is not glorious. I've been teaching confirmation for more than thirty years, and I don't have the hang of it yet. Ideas that seem fresh, stimulating, and important to me strike fourteen-year-olds as yesterday's mashed potatoes. I try to be electrifying, but eventually my patience runs thin with Kris, who is writing her boyfriend's name in pink magic marker on top of the Bible study for the week; and Chris, who stares at me hostilely week after week, making it clear that he is not in class of his own free will; and Cris, his chair tilted back onto two legs; and Kristin and Kirstin, who have slipped a copy of *Tiger Beat* magazine into the textbook and are now making ga-ga eyes at a picture of the latest heartthrob. (This is only mild exaggeration. I recently taught a confirmation class with five "Chrises" in it!) And then I blow the image I have been working on as the laid-back Bill Cosby of parish pastors and turn into the Incredible Hulk. The rest of the class is marked by loud bossy talking on my side, and sullen silence on theirs.

Nonetheless, each year I dare to dream that this will be the year, the year when I am bright, witty, exciting, and loving, and the students are cooperative, motivated, and eager to learn. But by the second session (or maybe the third), the line drives are whistling past my ears, and the Kristins are giggling as only teenage girls can, and I am wondering why I did not go into a more refined line of work—stock car racing, say.

In theory, I believe in confirmation, that pastoral and educational ministry of the church which we extend to adolescents as they traverse the painful road from childhood to adulthood. In theory, I believe in being tuned in to the needs, abilities, and interests of students. In theory, I believe in being responsive to their questions and encouraging them in the process of spiritual growth. Of course, in theory, I also believe in Santa Claus and the Easter Bunny.

But in practice, I'm not good at it. So I stand up in front of those teenagers with their hormones all aboil and try to convey a few basics about the faith. In our neck of the woods, confirmation is something you do for your children when they are in their early teens—on the order of orthodontia—whether you have brought them to Sunday school or not. Hence, many of my students come without much educational baggage concerning the faith once delivered to the saints. That being the case, I concentrate on the ABCs. No, Martin Luther King is *not* the same as Martin Luther. The Gospels are in the New Testament (the back third of your Bible) and tell the stories of Jesus. No, I do not believe that the Fifth Commandment refers to swatting mosquitoes. I will listen to you if you will listen to me. Maybe in between the Ten Commandments, the books of the Bible, and the history of the church, you will get the idea that the church *does* care about you a bit—and so do I, even if I do get mad and yell at you sometimes. My confirmation classes do not abound in sophisticated theology or touchy-feely group activities, but somehow we survive. And now and then there is a good night—or just a good ten minutes—when a few eyes light up, and a few tentative thoughts are shared, and I pick up just enough hope to keep me at it a little longer.

Why do I keep teaching confirmation year after year? There are three reasons. Reason #1 is simple and clear and probably holds true for you, too. Teaching confirmation is part of my call, part of my job description. If I did not teach confirmation, the congregation council would boil me in oil.

Reason #2 is Don Anderson. Reason #3 is John Kindschuh. Two pastors who some years ago put up with a smart-mouthed little know-it-all in their confirmation classes. He was there because his parents said that he had to be there, even though they had never bothered with pushing him into Sunday school. Those pastors talked to him about the meaning of faith on days when he didn't want to listen and patiently overlooked the wisecracks he made to John Hanson and his fumbling attempts to flirt with Mary Ann Harmer. He saw no reason to learn *The Small Catechism*, but they insisted that he be able to write and recite it from beginning to end, so he learned it. And when it was almost time for confirmation, the one who was then in charge told the smart-mouthed know-it-all that maybe, just maybe, God was calling *him* to be a pastor, an idea that seemed ridiculous at the time, but obviously started to make sense to me a few years later.

I do not love teaching confirmation, and I am not very good at it. But I will keep plugging along and dreaming of the perfect year because if I can do for one of my students what those two did for me, I will have a great deal to be proud of. And if I don't—well, survival is nothing to sneeze at when it comes to teaching confirmation.

When the Phone Rings

M Y PHONE DOES NOT RING AT 3:00 A.M. VERY OFTEN. WHEN it does, the call usually does not bring good news. It rang at 3:00 A.M. on a Monday morning not long ago. It was Terry, reporting to me on his twenty-month-old niece, Jennifer. Jennifer had become suddenly ill on Saturday night and was rushed to the hospital. By late Sunday afternoon she was in surgery. Surgery revealed the worst fears of the doctors. Her appendix had burst, probably Friday. Peritonitis had taken hold. By the time Terry had called me, Jennifer was being moved to a children's hospital thirty miles away. The doctor warned Jennifer's parents that she was so sick she might not survive the trip.

After a quick shower and shave, I was on the road. When I arrived at the children's hospital, the whole clan was gathered in the intensive care waiting room. Rod and Michelle, Jennifer's parent's, were in shock. They are young parents in their early twenties. I officiated at their wedding three years ago. Jennifer is their first child. I was soon told that Jennifer had survived the trip, but the doctors made it clear that she remained in very critical condition.

It took two hours for the doctors to thoroughly check Jennifer. When they were finished, the doctor in charge of the intensive-care unit laid it on the line for Rod and Michelle. Jennifer could die. She would be in critical condition for at least forty-eight hours. If she survived forty-eight hours, they could begin to have some hope for her.

The doctor left. Tears were shed. Conversation was labored. I offered prayer. And then there was nothing to do but wait. I stayed until about 8:00 A.M. On my way out of the hospital, I sought out the chaplain's office, where I found the Roman Catholic chaplain on duty. I told him about the case and asked him to look in on Jennifer's family during the day. He agreed.

I came back to the hospital on Monday afternoon, as well as Tuesday and Wednesday. Jennifer was an awful sight, a maze of tubes and wires and monitors. But she was hanging on. And Rod and Michelle, they were hanging on too. We would talk quietly, hold Jennifer's little hand, and share prayer.

On Wednesday, Rod and Michelle reported that the Roman Catholic chaplain wanted to see me. I paged him through his beeper, and in a few minutes we were sipping bitter black hospital coffee from Styrofoam cups in a conference room. We spent a few minutes getting better acquainted and discussing Jennifer and her family. I thanked him for faithfully calling on them. We talked of the partnership of hospital chaplain and local pastor. He thanked me for coming to the hospital.

I guess I looked a bit surprised when he said that, but then he said more: "We don't see many local pastors up here. It seems like a lot of pastors don't visit children in the hospital." I've thought a lot about that comment. I'd like to think that the chaplain was wrong—that pastors do visit children in the hospital but he just doesn't see them. But what if he was right? Why don't pastors visit children in the hospital? I can come up with two reasons:

#1: Pastors do not take children seriously as church members. It's great to have them in Sunday school and all that, but how do you talk to a child? What spiritual questions do they have and what spiritual needs are there for a pastor to meet? When there are already so many important people who go unseen and so many calls that go unmade, why waste your time calling on children?

#2: Pastors are personally threatened by sick children —especially when they are seriously ill. The pediatric

intensive care unit is a wonderful and terrible place. I admire the work that is done there, but I do not enjoy being there. It shakes me to look at those sick children. It stirs spiritual and theological questions in me that I've never had any good answers for. If you can go into a pediatric-intensive care unit and not feel touched, you're a stronger person than I am.

Now I don't want to give you the wrong impression. I'm no hero. To be starkly blunt about it, pastoral care is not my favorite part of the job. I do not claim to be of above-average faithfulness when it comes to hospital calling. If I had to choose between being a hospital chaplain and selling used cars, I'd go for the used cars in a minute. But I do call on members of the church who are hospitalized, and that does include children.

I call on children because this world can be a pretty scary place when you're a child, and it's an even scarier place when you're in the hospital. Children do not claim to understand how this whole medical business works. (Adults don't understand it any better, but we've learned to pretend we do.) All they know is that something doesn't feel right, and that, for all of the hard work and good will of the hospital staff, they are in a place that is definitely not home, nor is it the wonderful land of Oz.

Most of the children I call on know me from worship, Sunday school, and calls I've made in their homes. I'm a familiar face from outside the hospital. Some of the younger children confuse me with God. There is a time to set them straight on that. But if they are in a hospital bed, and get the idea from my visit that God was there with them and cares about them, we'll save the straightening out for another time.

I also call on children because children come with a parent or two, and parents are usually close by when a child is in the hospital. The parents are usually as upset as the child. The parents need the support of their church and their pastor during a traumatic time. When your child is hospitalized, it is *always* a traumatic time. It is a moment when persons are definitely open to ministry. Like it or not, it is our responsibility to be there to give it.

Jennifer made it. Three weeks later, on a Saturday, she was discharged from the hospital. And on Sunday she was at worship with her parents. Not everyone in our congregation knew what she had been through. But for those who did, it was a special moment. Rod and Michelle and I have a new kind of bond between us now, having shared the valley of the shadow. Jennifer may never remember her stay in the hospital or my visit to her, but I'm going to remember it for a long time. Thirteen years from now she'll be sitting in a confirmation class, and I'll be standing up there counting the days to retirement. When I look at her, I may well overlook her highjinks and remember the little girl who almost died.

As far as I am concerned, there is much more than enough "pastor bashing" going on these days. It would be disloyal of me to beat on my colleagues. I have confidence in the diligence of pastors. I believe that they do call on children in the hospital. I believe my chaplain friend was wrong about that. Pastors would not underestimate the importance of children in the Christian community. Pastors would not ignore their responsibility to minister to individuals and families in need. Pastors *do* visit children in the hospital.

Don't they?

Calling Isn't What It Used to Be

WHAT I FIRST EMBARKED ON THE SEA CRUISE OF PASTORAL ministry in the waning years of the Johnson presidency (Lyndon, not Andrew), my mentors taught me to structure my time in a simple, straightforward, traditional way.

Mornings were "office time," to be spent in my study doing sermon and lesson preparation, and the myriad tasks of parish administration. After lunch, it was time to get out on the road. Afternoons were spent calling. You would "hit the hospitals," of course, see a few shut-ins, and maybe drop in on some prospective members, an inactive family or two, or even an active family. You could count on the wife to be at home, at least, and it gave the whole family a good feeling to know that the pastor had stopped by. Evenings were for counseling, church meetings, or more calling.

It was a good system. It worked well. I never questioned it. I just assumed that this was the way God intended it to be. But I have found that the system doesn't work as well for me anymore. Maybe it does for you. If so, great. I envy you. It doesn't for me.

I get through the morning part just fine. I still plan on that being "office time." The problems begin after lunch. I still go to the hospitals, of course. However, in case you hadn't noticed, hospitalizations aren't what they used to be. When our first child was born in 1970, the average stay in the hospital for a mother with a new baby was five days. Now it is two. Surgeries which used to put someone in the hospital for five to seven days are now done on an outpatient basis, or with one overnight. Now when I get a call that so-and-so is in the hospital, I drop everything and go. If I wait for even a few hours, I might miss the person completely. This means that hospital calling does not take the time it used to.

So I go on to the shut-ins. But my absurdly youthful congregation only has two, and they can only take so much of me.

This, too, should leave me with lots of time to call on prospects, inactives, church families—maybe even go door-to-door, canvassing the neighborhood. However, we are a militantly suburban church. From 7:30 A.M. to 5:30 P.M. each day, the neighborhoods in our community look the way we all assume our denominational offices will look immediately after the Rapture, to put it in biblical language. It's like being in some sci-fi movie in which everyone has been sucked up into a giant spacecraft and delivered to Neptune, leaving only ghost towns behind. Women of today are not hanging around the house, hoping for the pastor to drop by for a cup of coffee and a slab of fresh-baked apple pie. I'd like to spend the afternoon calling—but it is almost impossible to find anyone to call on!

Evenings still fill up with meetings, counseling sessions, and other parish activities. But making an evening call in this place requires genius-level negotiating skills. "We'd love to see you, Pastor, but little Earl has karate lessons on Monday nights and we have to drive him back and forth, and I'll be flying back from Bismarck on Tuesday night, and Sally has an orthodontist appointment on Wednesday night, and Jim bowls on Thursday night, and we're going to the football game on Friday night." And so it goes, week after weary week.

According to the Harris Poll, the average American in 1973 had 26.2 hours of leisure time each week. In 1988, however, that "average American" had only 16.6 hours of leisure time. Moreover, what is "leisure time" for one member is "work time" for another, and a fair amount of our leisure time is as structured and frantic as work time.

A recent issue of *Time* magazine trumpeted the "rat race"–the time pressures modern Americans live with. For me, a pastoral call might seem like a chance to get to know people a little better, to extend ministry in a personal way. For the people I am calling on, it might be just one more appointment on an already-too-crowded calendar.

I usually look at this difficulty from the angle of the frustrated pastor who is trying to schedule a call. Recently, I came to the opposite perspective. Our family insurance agent called to make an appointment to sit down with us and review our property and auto coverage. I like our insurance agent. I have no complaints about the coverage we have. Reviewing your insurance is certainly a good idea. But I was not at all wild about the thought of giving up a rare and precious evening at home with the family to chat about insurance. I'm sure that plenty of folks feel about me the same way I felt about the insurance agent.

What I am now about to say is considered heretical in many quarters. Some of you will no doubt jump to the conclusion that the author should turn in his clerical collar for saying such a thing, that he and those like him are the reason for the decline of Christendom. I expect a fair share of fiery letters. But, as a wise man is reported to have said a few years back, "Here I stand. God help me."

Calling is a lower priority for me now than it used to be. (I can't believe I actually said that!) In this place, at this time, for this pastor, calling simply does not "work" the way it once did.

I would add very quickly that pastoral contacts are just as important as they ever were. But they are usually of a more random nature. The conversation at the grocery store or by the gas pumps, standing in the lobby before a school concert or washing out the coffee cups after a committee meeting, in the narthex after worship or in the parking lot after choir practice—these are the opportunities I have to "connect" with my people. The few words "on the fly" are important, and the telephone call has taken the place of the leisurely chat over pie and coffee. Rather than the formal visit in the home, we get together for a 5:00 A.M. breakfast at a local eatery, or under the ubiquitous golden arches for lunch.

Now before you send off that angry letter, be informed that I do make calls. I call faithfully on the sick and shut-in, the elderly, and the bereaved. I call on as many prospective members as I can. When the need arises and I know about it, I'll be there. Personal contact with the members of this church is absolutely crucial to me. I take advantage of every opportunity for such contact.

But I don't do as much calling as I once did, and I certainly do not do as much calling as previous generations of pastors have done. It's not that I dislike calling. I get a particular kick out of calling on prospects.

But at this time, in this place, for this pastor and these people, calling simply doesn't work like it used to. That's too bad—but it is reality.

So when afternoon comes anymore, I might actually be found at my desk, polishing the Sunday sermon or writing my column for the church newsletter. I won't feel as guilty as I would have ten years ago about not being out calling. A little bit guilty. But not as guilty.

Developers and Scripture Study

THE PICTURES OF THE NEW RESORT DEVELOPMENT LOOK LOVELY. Cozy modern cabins nestled up to a tree-lined lake with a golf course stretching out toward the horizon. Happy boaters with stringers full of keepers. A family gathered around the fireplace. Cordial neighbors enjoying a barbecue together. The good life.

I could sample that good life for free. They will give me two nights free in one of their cottages, a boat to use, and unlimited access to a golf course. All I have to do is schedule a visit, and include in that visit a little time to hear what is promised to be a low-key presentation about the advantages of "buying in" on one of the cabins on a time-share basis.

It sounds harmless. But I always say *no*. I say no because I know myself. I know that my sales resistance is not always that great, that I can sometimes be captivated even by a low-key presentation and that I could easily be seduced into buying. In fact, I cannot afford to buy. But if I listen to the presentation, I might. So I am better off passing up the wonderful free offer to protect myself from getting drawn in.

Now, let's put aside my reluctance to accept the offer and talk about adult Bible study.

The results are in. If there is one programmatic element common to virtually all thriving congregations, it is a strong program of adult Bible study. We all know that, so if we want our congregations to be strong, we will see to it that the adults of the congregation are studying the Bible on a regular basis.

I believe that, and I am happy to believe it. Like most pastors, I delight in Bible study and enjoy teaching adults, engaging them in dialogue about the great teachings and truths of the Bible.

However, I cannot say that adult Bible study is a main cash crop of my congregation. One group of six to eight men meets regularly for breakfast and Bible study at 6:00 A.M. On Monday morning, a group of comparable size wrestles with Search materials. In the last few months, a small group has been meeting in homes for Bible study two evenings each month. Two of our women's circles faithfully work their way through the studies published by the Women of the Evangelical Lutheran Church in America.

But the plain truth is that we do not have a significant number of adults engaged in Bible study on a regular basis. My partner in ministry and I talk about this all the time. Both of us are willing to make adjustments in our own schedules to work with Bible study groups. There are also competent lay teachers present in the congregation. But so far we have not been able to motivate any large number of people to commit themselves to a regular Bible study. We are both frustrated. The two of us *perceive* adult Bible study as a major need of this congregation. But the people of the congregation do not seem to *feel* the need. Therefore, in spite of all of our best attempts, adult Bible study in groups is not happening on a significant scale.

Needless to say, we wonder why. When we ask people why, they usually tell us that they would really like to be in a Bible study group but that their schedules—jammed to the gills with bowling leagues, and aerobic classes, and PTA meetings—simply won't allow it. Now and then we might even get up the nerve to be confrontational about it, and ask them about their life priorities, and how these priorities are reflected by their schedules. But the extent to which we can use that technique of motivation by guilt is limited.

So why are the people of this congregation reluctant to commit themselves to serious adult Bible study? While schedule does have something to do with it, I believe that there is more to it than that. Let's go back to the very beginning and my reluctance to listen to the spiels of developers.

As I said, I do not listen to those spiels because I am afraid that I might get drawn in further than I really want to go. I wonder if our people do not feel the same way about Bible study. I wonder if they do not recognize the incendiary power of God's word, a power to revolutionize values and change lives. To the "ordinary person," the Bible can seem like one of those black holes the astronomers talk about, blessed with such an intense gravitational pull that it draws in anything or anyone that comes close, with no means of escape. To study the Bible would be to come close to its pull, and face the danger of having life altered in a revolutionary way. That is not an attractive thought to most people. They rather like their lives the way they are. Unless and until something happens to create a great *dis*-ease with life as it is, they will be committed to keeping it that way. Their reluctance to get involved in Bible study is *not* an indication that they do not take the Bible seriously. It is a way of saying that they fear the Bible and the impact it could have on their lives if they allowed it to. So they do not.

If my theory is correct, then the challenge we face is that of enabling people to overcome their fear and venture ahead in faith. I wish I could tell you that I know exactly how to do that, but I do not. If I knew, I would be getting rich teaching others how to do it. And I would not need to put down for you in black-and-white this confession of failure on my part.

For this is exactly what it feels like. I know that the

people of this congregation would find their faith enhanced and strengthened by regular study of the Bible. I know that this congregation would be much stronger if more of the members of the congregation were involved in Bible study on a regular basis. I know that I, as a pastor of this church, should find ways to make that happen. But I haven't found the ways yet.

The materials produced by the church report to us regularly on the positive results of adult Bible study in congregations. We are urged to have such programs in our congregations. We are offered the models of congregations where fine programs are taking place.

But this congregation is not one of those models. Far from it. You won't see our picture in any book, which is yet another reason that I am grateful for a God of grace, who forgives me for not having a bang-up program of adult Bible study. It is much harder for me to forgive myself.

"McKinley's Laws"

THE FIRST SYNOD/DISTRICT CONVENTION/ASSEMBLY I ATTENDED after ordination was held in the ballroom of a magnificent hotel. At one high moment in the gathering, the presiding officer summoned to the front of the hall for recognition pastors celebrating the twenty-fifth, thirtieth, fortieth, and fiftieth anniversaries of their ordinations.

As they doddered to the front, I remember marveling at them. At that point in my life, twenty-five years seemed virtually as long as fifty years. I had only been alive for twenty-five years at the time! These guys (and they were all guys) had lasted for twenty-five years as pastors! Some of them even more! What would it be like to be a pastor for twenty-five years, for heaven's sake? These had to be really old people.

I have particular reason for remembering that moment these days. You see, if my synod chooses to do that same sort of thing this year, I will be one of those doing the doddering. As of 1997, I've been a parish pastor for thirty years. Scary thought.

Having spent more than twenty-five years at this pastoring trade, I am now, of course, an expert. As an expert, I am prepared to share with you twelve lessons I have learned about parish ministry that you never learned in seminary. You don't know these things when you are first ordained. After twenty-five years, you know that they are true. Call them "McKinley's Laws."

Law #1

That person who sticks his or head into your office and asks, "Do you have a minute?" really wants at least an hour.

Law #2

The pitiful wretch who comes off the street, tugs at your heart strings with a touching story of personal tragedy, and asks to "borrow" money—promising on his sainted mother's grave to pay you back—will not pay you back. Maybe you will want to give the money anyway, but do not expect to see it again in this lifetime.

Law #3

When you prepare a sermon you're really proud of, it will fall flat. On the other hand, the sermons you believe to be complete duds will be enthusiastically received.

Law #4

Congregation council meetings will take longer and accomplish less than you expect. (Never try to tell your spouse ahead of time how long you expect a council meeting to take. You will always be wrong. The ones you expect to be over in one hour will take three. The meetings you expect to take three hours will take one. The council members who are most eager to end the official meeting will then spend one hour huddled in small groups in the parking lot.)

Law #5

Your best intentions to make weddings a holy and sacred time of worship will invariably be thwarted.

Law #6

The bright and shining young pastoral stars who hit your synod with a bang and assume significant leadership positions in short order will be peddling fraternal insurance within a few years.

Law #7

If you come into the church office dressed casually one day each year, an emergency will occur on that day and you will wish you were wearing more "official" looking clothing. (One of my mentors taught me some years ago to always keep a black clergy shirt in my closet. I've used that shirt more than once.)

Law #8

There are no miracle cures. There is no program that will instantly solve your problems with stewardship, evangelism, Christian education, or other areas. The congregation that currently gives 2.5 percent of its income will not become a tithing congregation next year, no matter what you do. Hard, steady, relentless work can make a difference over time.

Law #9

The people who are most eager to become your dear and intimate friends when you arrive in a new parish are not to be trusted. They probably have an ax to grind. Within one year you will either have become their tool or totally alienated them.

Law #10

Stepping away from the local congregation for just one law, the same people will bring substantially the same resolutions to the synod assembly each year. If you move to another synod, you will find that your new synod will have similar people to take their place. The resolutions and the speeches on the convention floor will be unchanged.

Law #11

People will always tease you about your ability to control the weather. You cannot. However, if your area is desperately in need of rain, try scheduling either an outdoor wedding or a church picnic. This will usually bring rain.

Law #12

You will regularly foul up. You will know the kind of pastor you want to be, but you will not live up to that vision. (See Romans 7.) The congregation will regularly disappoint you. They will resist new ideas. They'll stay away from worship to watch a football game. They will fail to carry out the tasks they have volunteered to do. They will remove any doubts you might have had about the power of original sin. But somehow the Holy Spirit will work through your imperfect ministry in that imperfect congregation to change the world with the good news of Jesus Christ. You might not see the changes. But never doubt for a minute that they are taking place.

I hope you young whippersnappers appreciate my generosity in sharing this knowledge with you. When I was first ordained, those gnarled veterans of twenty-five to fifty years of ministry really couldn't teach me much about ministry, even though they tried, since I already knew so much. Today's "veterans" (like myself) are much wiser than yesterday's veterans were. Obviously.

Don't applaud, just send money.

Danielle, Gertrude, and Baptism

I AM COUNTING ON GOD TO HAVE A SENSE OF HUMOR. IF GOD does not have a good sense of humor, I'll be in deep trouble on that great gettin' up mornin'. Of course, I'll be in deep trouble, anyway, but I can trust that to God's forgiving grace. This will depend first of all upon the divine sense of humor. Then grace.

It has to do with baptizing a Cabbage Patch doll named Gertrude.

Danielle is four. She is the executive older sister of two younger brothers. Not long ago we baptized the newer of the brothers. A couple of weeks later, Danielle's father approached me after worship on a Sunday morning with a somewhat sheepish look on his face. "Danielle would like to know if you would baptize Gertrude," he asked. As strange as this sounds, I knew who he was talking about. You seldom see Danielle without Gertrude.

Danielle had been so taken by her baby brother's baptism that she had decided her own "baby," Gertrude, should be baptized. In the prior week, she had talked of it often both to her parents and to Gertrude. Now it was Sunday morning, and she and Gertrude were ready, if I was willing.

I am by nature a stodgy and conservative Lutheran pastor. I take baptism very seriously. That's why we offer baptism classes for the parents of the fifty to seventy children we baptize each year. As joyful as it is, baptism is serious business, and should be taken seriously. As a rule, baptism is for human beings claimed by the grace of God.

Now I have *blessed* all sorts of things in my time: church buildings, organs, paraments, homes. I said an invocation once for a horse show. On one particularly weird day, I blessed a group of motorcycles.

But there is a clear difference between blessing and baptizing, and I am much pickier about baptism. I do not go around casually baptizing dolls. If the doll's "parents" want to play church and baptize the dolls themselves, fine. Our baptismal practice is limited to living, breathing, human beings.

But Danielle is a sweetheart, and she wanted Gertrude baptized. I could tell by what her parents told me and by the look on Danielle's face that this was not just a little game but something she took with all the seriousness a four-year-old can muster. So I agreed to baptize Gertrude, and marched up to the font, filled with the paranoid fear that a gaggle of systematic theologians would come stumbling in just as I was pouring water on Gertrude's head.

I amended the baptismal service as we went along. Danielle promised to read Bible storybooks to Gertrude, and to bring her to worship sometimes. Danielle's parents (Gertrude's grandparents) and brothers (Gertrude's uncles) watched respectfully, insofar as you can watch the baptism of a Cabbage Patch doll respectfully. One of our Altar Guild women even got into the act, lifting Danielle up so she could get a better look at what was happening. The service was over in a few minutes. Gertrude did not cry, I'll say that for her. Danielle was pleased. She took all this baptism business more seriously than some other "parents" do. Verily, Gertrude is at worship every Sunday. While I did not add her to the roll of baptized members of the church, I am considering sending her a pledge card when the Every Member Response rolls around again. In that respect, she would do no worse than some actual members we already have.

When I baptized Gertrude, I pictured this as a simple little transaction between Danielle, her parents, and me. No such luck. Ever since that day, people have been coming up to me with cracks like "I hear you're baptizing dolls these days." What can I say? I did, indeed, baptize one doll. But I'm not going to get into the habit of doll-baptizing, and it would not bother me if word of this sacramental travesty did not travel far.

But at that particular moment in time there was this little girl, and she knew somehow that baptism was something very important, that it was a sign of being part of God's family. And she wanted that for her doll, and I did not have it in me to say no. Maybe all of this cheapens baptism, or trivializes it. Perhaps it offends and upsets my theological betters, of whom there are many. Maybe it leaves me looking like a boob, a clown, a spineless marshmallow unwilling to stand up for the confessional heritage of the church. I grant all of those things as genuine possibilities.

But I am willing to risk all of that, because I know how much this "pseudo-baptism" meant to Danielle, and because I believe in taking children seriously. I like to think that years from now, when Danielle is in fact the parent of a real human child that she will remember the day we baptized Gertrude and will take the baptism of her human child just as seriously. I hope she will. In spite of my theological training, I still can't help picturing heavenly realities in earthly ways. So I picture myself standing, as people in jokes are always standing, at the gates of heaven. Saint Peter is checking "the book."

"You're the guy that baptized the doll?"

"Right."

"The Boss got a kick out of that one."

And as the gates of heaven swing open, who is standing there on the inside? Gertrude.

I'll admit it's schmaltzy. But it's the kind of schmaltz that keeps me getting out of bed in the morning.

Cellular Blessings and Curses

L ET ME SEE THE HANDS OF ALL OF THOSE OUT THERE WHO HAVE cellular telephones in their cars.

Congratulations, those of you with your hands sticking up in the air. (But don't you feel at least a little bit foolish sitting there wherever you are sitting with your hand over your head?) You are truly with it and modern, out on the cutting edge of pastoral technology. If the cellular telephone in your car also includes a fax machine, you are eligible for election to the College of Communication Cardinals. And if your cellular phone is actually so mobile that you carry it with you wherever you go, prepare yourself to be considered for the papacy of the church progressive.

The efficiency mavens of my congregation have encouraged me to look into getting a cellular telephone for my car, one I could obediently tote around with me all the time, but I have not succumbed.

I can see the advantages. If Ms. Miniver goes into cardiac arrest while I am wheeling my way to the monthly meeting of the Pastors Union, I could straightway adjust my course and head to the hospital. If the morning has been busy and I have eight telephone calls to return, I could make good use of the time it takes to drive to the nursing home for a round of visits. If my buddy Mordecai hears the latest poop on who is being called to Old Fourth Lutheran Church, he'd be able to get to me right away, thus sparing us both a two-day game of telephone tag. Verily, a cellular phone would make it possible for my office to be in constant communication with me, and I with them. How inspiring!

Still, I have not yet acquired the cellular telephone, and

it is not just because I am, to use the technical word for my condition, cheap. It is also because I cling to the old-fashioned notion that there are some places a telephone is not meant to go.

Example #1: The Golf Course

Last summer I played an invitational golf tournament that included a number of captains of industry. They had their telephones in their golf carts with them. Every now and again I would see one of them in animated conversation on the telephone, while the rest of their group stood by polishing their wedges. Perhaps the fate of great nations or the course of American industry depended on those telephone calls. Still, couldn't they have waited until they got back to the club house?

Example #2: Restaurants

The other day I had lunch with a friend in a modest restaurant. At the table next to ours there were two be-suited men with briefcases. When they sat down, each reached into his briefcase and pulled out his telephone, which he put on the table just to the left of his fork. (The etiquette books say this is where the telephone belongs.) In the course of the meal, each answered several telephone calls from someone. Indeed, at one point in the meal both of them were sitting there face to face, food cooling between them, talking on the telephone. Maybe they had called each other. Not for me, thanks.

Example #3: Meetings

As of the time of writing this has not yet happened to me, but I have the uneasy feeling that it's only a matter of time. Picture yourself at the monthly luncheon meeting of the conference clergy. Picture pastors arriving bearing their own personal telephones. Picture the endless ringing of these telephones. Indeed, picture the insecure among us who have instructions with their secretaries to call at the meeting at such-and-such a time, just to prove that they are as important as the next pastor.

Example #4: My Car

My car is a little sanctuary on wheels, a place where I can sing or scream, listen to Montovani or the Grateful Dead, carry on a mental debate with Rush Limbaugh, keep up with the Minnesota Twins, think deep thoughts, plan sermons, or even pray. (Don't worry. I do not close my eyes and bow my head in prayer while driving. I used to have a friend who did. However, his driving was so bad all the time that the difference was not discernible.) I am not willing to sacrifice my sanctuary just to take telephone calls from folks trying to sell me aluminum siding, or to place a pizza order while on the road.

My track record in resisting the lures of modern technology is not good. I traditionally begin by lamenting the sorry state of humankind as reflected by the encroachment of new-fangled gadgets, and by saying, "Not me, no sir, no way, no thanks." Then, a few years later, I give in and take one more halting step into the modern world. Thus it was the answering machine, the computer, the fax machine.

Thus it will probably be with the cellular telephone. I may even have broken down by the time this article appears in print.

Still, worrying about such things is one of my hobbies, so I worry. I worry about our inability to escape from work to enjoy some simple leisure. I worry that we are so willing to let the telephone intrude in our lives and our dealings with each other. I worry that an ever-present telephone robs us of much-needed sanctuary. I know that I need pieces of time in my life when I can be confident that the phone *won't* ring, and I can simply be alone with myself.

Finally, I worry that acquiring a telephone to carry around with me all the time would go to my head and inflate my ego. It could be a way of saying, "I am so important that the world needs to be able to reach me at any time. Catastrophe will certainly result if people cannot reach me twenty-four hours a day, seven days a week, 365 days a year."

I do not want to say that. I do not want to think that. I'll keep passing on the cellular telephone until I can resist it no longer. When I get one, I will publish the number for you, and you can call me up now and then to remind me not to get too big for my britches.

(P.S. I do know that my bishop has a cellular phone in his car. Don't take it this personally, Your Holiness!)

What Do We Do
When the World Doesn't
Tell Us What to Do?

I T WAS MY FIRST SESSION OF PREMARITAL COUNSELING WITH A young couple. The bride was a member of my congregation, but the groom was a stranger. In trying to get acquainted with him, I asked what he did for a living.

He earnestly explained that he had trouble holding a regular job. He was deeply involved in the local volunteer ambulance program and in the local volunteer fire department. He carried a beeper with him at all times to accept those calls, and never let a regular paying job interfere with his emergency calls. When the beeper sounded, he went.

In reflecting back on his first marriage, he ventured the opinion that it began to fail during the honeymoon. The day after the wedding, he and his bride were driving through a major city. They came upon a five-alarm fire. He dropped his bride at a motel, pulled his fire gear out of the trunk, and went to the fire. For two days.

He was sure that the second marriage would be more successful, for wife number two shared his interest in fires and ambulances. Besides, they were to be married on the anniversary of what he considered to be the most exciting and fulfilling day of his life—the day a tornado hit our town and he had more than twenty-four hours worth of emergencies.

Now I for one am grateful that there are people in this world to staff the ambulances and fire departments. I would not be good at this. Any fire larger than the one in a fireplace makes me anxious. The sight of blood makes me sick to my stomach. Praise God for the variety of gifts!

At the same time, it strikes me a little strange to build your life so much around emergencies and catastrophes that you cannot cope with ordinary days and orderly work. The groom-to-be had a problem with that. When there was no fire to fight, no life to save, he didn't know quite what to do with himself. That attitude can be a problem for pastors also.

Whenever the topic of time management comes up in a group of clergy, the initial speakers advocate planning, order, discipline, scheduling, regular time off, that sort of thing. After a few of them have had a chance to say their piece, the resident martyr speaks up.

"I don't understand this talk about time management. We're *not* called to be managers. [*Hiss! Boo!*] We're *not* called to be executives. [*Hiss! Boo!*] We're called to be servants. I can't plan for my time. I can't schedule time off. I never know when *my people* might need me. I have to be at their disposal all the time. You never know when there might be an emergency."

This has the effect of making everyone else feel guilty and unworthy of the ministry for even suggesting that the time of a pastor could be ordered, managed, and scheduled.

But really now—isn't ministry something more than answering fire bells? Don't we also have to do some ordinary, orderly work to be effective shepherds for our flock? Don't we have to put some order in our own lives for the sake of our own sanity, our own families, the whole broad spectrum of our parish responsibilities?

Admittedly, emergencies do occur; and when they occur, we want to be there. There is an old adage that says, "When death comes, the pastor goes," and none of us would ever dispute that. My phone rings sometimes, and I drop whatever it is that I am doing to race to a hospital or a home or do some emergency counseling. That happens to all of us in the ministry, and we would never turn away those calls.

But really now, how often does that happen to you? Does it really happen often enough to justify throwing any attempt at time management out the window on the grounds that "you never know when there might be an emergency"? Maybe I'm callous and heartless, but emergencies certainly don't happen to me that often. While I've never bothered to keep count, I doubt that I've ever had more than a half-dozen genuine *emergencies* requiring my immediate presence in any one calendar year.

In truth, while we never hope for emergencies, they do bring a measure of ego gratification with them. When one is able to help an individual or a family through a time of trauma, there is a certain sense of satisfaction and fulfillment. What's more, having people dependent on you makes you feel important. And imagine yourself at a clergy meeting. The phone rings. Silence descends as the group waits to see for whom the bell tolls. When it tolls for thee, and you have to go deal with an emergency, you sure do show up the rest of those pastors whose people don't need them nearly as much as your people need you.

It is dramatic to convince our colleagues and our congregations that we are forever answering emergency calls. But I have trouble believing that any pastor really gets that many emergency calls. Trying to convince other people and ourselves that our lives must be built around answering the alarm may be just a way of avoiding the daily responsibilities of life, which, while not overly dramatic, may be just as important.

Having relocated myself, I have no way of knowing how marriage is working out for the firefighter and his bride. I hope that they are still getting the same thrill out of answering the alarm bell. But I also hope that they are finding a satisfying way to get along when there is no emergency, no way of deafening themselves to the din within by responding to the din without.

That is also our adventure as pastors. When there is an emergency, we know what to do, and I am confident that most of us do it well. The real test of our ministry comes at those moments when the fire bell isn't ringing.

THE PASTOR'S FOIBLES

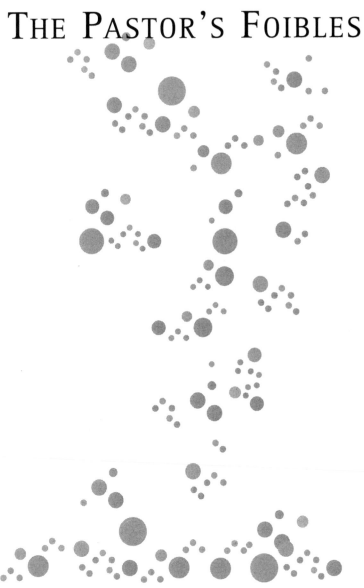

Old, Familiar Lessons

CHURCH GROWTH EXPERTS SUGGEST THAT A CONGREGATION would do well to identify its "niche," that portion of the population that it best serves. Sometimes I think that ours might be those critics who say that they don't believe in organized religion. We do believe in organized religion, but we don't always practice it very well.

Take last year's Labor Day weekend, for example. The adventure began when I perused the bulletin and realized that I had selected an opening hymn for worship on that Sunday which even I did not know. I have no idea how I did it. But I did.

Now I am a typical pastor, which means that now and then I take some flak for picking unfamiliar hymns. But I never pick a hymn that is unfamiliar to me, and I never pick one that might be unfamiliar to the congregation as an opening hymn. Furthermore, I stick to familiar standards on holiday weekends. This was clearly a mistake.

So I selected a different, more familiar hymn, put a note to the organist on the organ bench, and got out the ladder and changed the number on the hymnboard. I wrote a note to myself to announce this change in advance.

I did announce it at the beginning of the first service. Pay attention to the hymnboard, not the bulletin, I told the people. But my ever-efficient ushers had noticed that the hymnboard did not agree with the bulletin, so they had already changed the hymnboard back to the original number to make it conform to the bulletin. Let's say this created a bit of confusion. By the time the second service started, the hymnboard was the way I wanted it to be. But then things really started to fall apart.

As it is to be expected on a holiday weekend, the

assigned acolytes did not show up, and I neglected to tell the hastily recruited replacements to light the paschal candle for the baptism that would be taking place at that service. They didn't. So, during the first hymn, I dispatched one of them to perform that holy duty. Then, during the first hymn, I noticed three things:

#1: I had forgotten to place the baptismal candle on the font.

#2: The altar guild had neglected to recover one of the stacks of communion trays on the altar.

#3: Only two of the three assigned communion assistants were present for the service.

Well, the communion trays stayed uncovered. During the second hymn, I walked piously down to the font and got the baptismal candle. And during the third hymn, I went back into the sacristy and wrote a quick note to our youth director, who was seated in the congregation, asking her to fill in as the third communion assistant. However, she had only been on our staff for two months at the time and never handled this duty before.

When the ushers came forward to get the offering plates, I handed the note to one of them and whispered, "Give this note to Sarah." He looked back at me and said, "Who's Sarah?" Luckily his partner did know who Sarah was. The note was delivered.

When Sarah got the note, she slipped out to get an alb and some instructions from the more experienced communion assistants. But one of them was already wearing the one alb that fits Sarah properly, even though it was much too short for him. As a result, when the assistants marched to the altar at communion time, he looked like he was wearing a mini-alb, while Sarah was dragging a train behind her—a situation somewhat hazardous to balance. Nonetheless, no tragedy transpired, and the sacrament was more-or-less rightly administered.

Fortunately it was a holiday weekend. Not many of the saints were on hand to witness this debacle. On that particular Sunday, we certainly violated the old canon about things being done "decently and in order."

But there was one family at worship with us for the first time. When they came through my line at the end of the service, I was bracing myself to apologize to them, ready to tell them that we are usually more organized than we were that particular Sunday.

I never got the speech out of my mouth. "What a wonderful service!" the woman said. "Everything seemed so warm, so spontaneous, so relaxed." Then her husband chimed in. "We haven't been to church in years. Churches always seemed so sterile and strict. But this church is an exciting place to be. We'll be back next Sunday."

It makes you stop and think. As a believer in and advocate of good organization and planning, I had found that service disastrous. I hope I never have to live through another one like it again. I'm not sure I could live through very many. But to these unchurched people, it seemed warm, cordial, and inviting.

I relearned two old and familiar lessons that day. First of all, I relearned that, as the hymn puts it, "God moves in a mysterious way, [God's] wonders to perform." Even though all of our organizational systems seemed to be breaking down at the same time on that day, God's grace broke through. Grace does not depend upon us, upon our plans, upon the excellence of our liturgy or the polish of our organization. (Which is not to say that we should not strive for excellence in liturgy and polish in organization. There is something to be said for excellence and polish.) The Holy Spirit blows wherever it darn well pleases. And sometimes it blows in places we would never expect it to be.

Second, I relearned one of the basic principles of ministry in this surprising world.

You never know.

The Passing of a Quiet Month

I T HAS BEEN A QUIET MONTH FOR THIS LITTLE FLOCK GATHERED between the shores of two lakes with the imaginative names "Crooked" and "Round."

Easter passed, and as soon as it passed, worship attendance dropped like a stone. (Yes, there is a considerable gap between the time I write these words and the time you read them.) The Minnesota mind thinks of Easter as the beginning of spring, and pilgrimages to "the Lake" begin immediately, even though there is still ice on the lake. We have our priorities in order. Getting away for the weekend is important. Worship is optional.

Of course, when attendance drops, so does the income. We haven't been doing all that well anyway, and as summer has drawn nearer, we've slipped further and further into the red.

A gung-ho Long-Range Planning (LRP) team has been at work trying to shape a mission plan for the next three years. It is a good group, and their work is energizing to me. That is, most of the time.

Following good "process," the LRP team polled the congregation on the Sunday after Easter, trying to get some reading on their evaluation of the current state of things in this neck of the woods. When the LRP team met on Tuesday night, the agenda was an analysis of the feedback from the congregation. There were, of course, ecstatic lovers of the congregation and caustic critics, too. One respondent rated us low in every area, and then, at the end, wrote this comment: "This would be a good place to start a real church."

Yes, he did sign his name. He and I have been bugging each other for eleven years now. As far as he is concerned, the Assemblies of God is a real church. As long as we are not that, we will never be. But his wife is on our staff, so he sticks around.

I was not surprised by his comment. But, I must admit, I was hurt. I was hurt because, while I would not be the first to say that we are far from perfect, I would also not want to say that we are totally hopeless. And I was hurt because of the impact his comment had on the LRP team. They felt hurt. I could hear it in their voices. They joked about the comment, but I could also hear that they were stung by the comment, and feeling bad for me. So there we sat, feeling bad for each other.

We've also been at odds with our neighbors and the local city council for the last month over the lofty theological issue of road access to our parking lot. The city council and the neighbors believe that such access is optional. As a matter of fact, they believe they'd be better off without it. But we have a bias in favor of people being able to get into the parking lot, so we've been holding our ground.

By default (and probably by mistake), I have become the general of our army in this little war. I am the one the mayor calls. I am the one the neighbors castigate. I am the one who is expected to be able to state the church's position. I am the one who has to keep our little army in line, encouraging the faint of heart and reining in the zealots.

Perhaps my theological education was flawed, but seminary did not teach me to do this kind of thing. As a matter of fact, I even cling to the antiquated notion that I was called to deal with some matters that are loftier than parking lot access. I do not find it particularly uplifting to spend several hours out of every day discussing the parking lot. We do have a parking lot. We do need a parking lot. People need to be able to get into the parking lot.

When you go much further than this, I start to glaze over. But there is a war to be fought, and I have been conscripted into the officer corps.

It was a cold, rainy, and dark month in Minnesota. For a variety of reasons, the period of time from Easter to Memorial Day is usually the most hectic time of the year for me, so there were not many opportunities for me to enjoy leisure. Now and then I got a look at the sun through my windshield or my office window, but when I was free to go outside, "the rains came down and the floods came up," as an old Sunday school song puts it.

Last Sunday, we tried to whip up the troops with a mission festival. The joint was jumping with "intergenerational education activities" designed to educate people about the mission of the church in this country and around the world. It was great fun watching the little ones stamp barefooted on wet sand as they considered African brickmaking.

We had as our special guests a couple who recently returned to this country after nearly twenty years of service as missionaries in Africa. They displayed African artifacts and presented a dialogue sermon about their work in Africa among nomadic peoples of the sub-Saharan region.

The first time I listened to the dialogue, I simply drank it in. The second time through I sat and looked at the congregation. I thought of these missionaries extending the gospel to people who were often malnourished, to those whose living was barely subsistence. Their whole way of life was being threatened. Just to add to the challenge, 99 percent of the people in the region served were followers of Islam. These missionaries did not serve people who retreated to "the Lake" for the weekend. They did not have a Long-Range Planning team. They did not fight with the city council and neighbors about a parking lot. They simply shared the gospel in word and deed.

Then all of a sudden, there I was feeling guilty. While my life and my ministry do have their stresses and strains, I have things pretty easy. The congregation I serve is strong, well-established, and (most of the time) supportive. I am surrounded by a good support system. I can get down sometimes about the little struggles we have around here. That is inevitable. But when I start slipping into humankind's least attractive emotion, self-pity, I'm in big trouble. And that is precisely where I have been.

I thanked the missionaries when they left for the message they brought to the congregation, but I really meant to say thanks for the message they brought to me. Since last Sunday, I've been doing a little better, thanks. Today the sun is out, and this morning I played eighteen holes of golf with a good friend. He told me about the pressures he's been feeling, and I told him about the pressures I've been feeling, and we laughed, and hit the golf ball, and walked, and when it was done, we sat down and had lunch together. And it was good. And life was good. Not always easy. But good.

So that's what's been happening between the lakes "Crooked" and "Round," where all the meetings are long, all of the people are opinionated, and all of the pastors are about average.

The Seasons of a Cleric's Life

WHEN MY SON WAS THREE OR FOUR, THE TWO OF US HAD A little tradition we both enjoyed. At the end of worship each Sunday, he would sneak over to the center aisle of the church. Then, when I came walking down the aisle during the recessional, he would step out, take my hand, and walk to the back of the church with me.

Harry, a friend in the congregation, always enjoyed seeing Kirk and me hand-in-hand. In time, Harry's employer required him to relocate, and he left the congregation. When we had our last visit together, Harry said that he was happy to be leaving the congregation at that time for one reason.

"The time will come when Kirk won't want to walk hand-in-hand with you anymore. That will be a sad day. I'm glad I won't be here to see it."

Harry was right. The time did come, and it was a sad day for me, if not for Kirk.

I remembered that conversation recently during a family night at home. My wife was reading to the children, and I was both sitting as a part of the family group and mentally outside that setting, looking at the five of us together in the living room. I marveled at how the children were growing and changing.

The last ten years have gone by quickly, each year a little faster than the one before. The next ten years could go even faster. Then our children will be grown and gone from under our roof. What will they remember then about their father? Am I being the kind of father they need to help them mature into being the people God created them to be?

At about that time I read an article by Gaylord Noyce in which he talked about "The Seasons of a Cleric's Life."

The article included this quote from a female pastor: "When male groups or mixed clergy are together they talk about many things, but *never* about an issue that dominates much of our conversation when women pastors meet: how to cope with family responsibilities and the job at the same time."

My experience comes close to bearing that out. While I cannot honestly say that I have never been part of a conversation about family life among pastors, the occasions have been rare. When they have happened, it has usually been in the context of bemoaning the impossibility of the whole undertaking.

Here is where the conversation turns particularly worrisome. My experience seems to suggest that, if we conclude that it is impossible to be both a responsible member of the family circle and an adequate pastor, then we usually conclude that the church, not the family, must take top priority. If the church council meeting and the school concert or the Little League championship game come on the same night, we go to the council meeting.

I identify with those pastors who agonize over those situations. I do the same. To tell the truth, I would probably decide for the church council meeting myself, after stewing about it a bit first.

But I wonder about those who do *not* agonize at all in such moments, who automatically take it for granted that the church must always take first place and the family second place. Perhaps they experience less stress in life than those who struggle with the question, but I'm not convinced that they are better off.

I doubt that their families are better off. Perhaps their families have learned to live with the situation. Perhaps their spouses are rugged and independent and keep the family going in their absence. Perhaps their spouses even agree that, for a pastor, the church must take precedence over the family. Perhaps their children have come to terms with the consistent absenteeism of father or mother, like the children in a single-parent family. In effect, they do live in a single-parent family.

Then again, perhaps not. Perhaps spouses are swallowing a lot of anger and frustration and sadness and loneliness, rather than speaking up against "a sacred calling." Perhaps children are growing up thinking of the church mainly as something that took father and mother away from them at crucial moments. Perhaps the pastors themselves are cutting themselves off from love and support and humanity and some of the greatest joys life has to offer.

There are two easy ways of ridding oneself of the tension between family and profession:

#1: Give up church.

#2: Give up family.

As most of us are not willing to do either, we will have to continue to wrestle with these conflicting pressures on life. But our lives will be out of balance if the same side wins the fight every time.

I touched on some of these topics in the first column I ever wrote for *Lutheran Partners* magazine, back in February 1980. After that column appeared, I received a letter from and grand and highly respected pastor who had retired not long before that.

"I was a model pastor," he said. "I was a slave to the church. I served the people. I neglected my family. I was a fool." He was highly respected. He had served a large church. His people loved him. He was a leader in the denomination. He retired in a blaze of glory. His verdict on his own life and ministry: "I was a fool."

I would be a little kinder. Many of you have a spouse and perhaps children to summon you to responsible life in the family. If that is not enough, then think—think hard—about the words of my correspondent:

"I was a fool."

Pastors to Each Other

WEDNESDAY MORNING, 7:30 A.M. A COMFORTABLE, MODERN church on the outer edge of suburbia. Our clergy cluster group is gathering. Every other Wednesday we come together for ninety minutes to discuss the lectionary texts for ten days hence and our lives in our congregations.

The group varies a bit from time to time. This morning there are nine of us. Judy is the host. She is assistant pastor in this congregation, and will lead the lectionary discussion. Jake is a former seminary faculty member who yearned to return to the parish, and did. Pete, the district dean, and Mark, his young associate. Linda, a middle-aged woman who went back to seminary after her children were grown, now on the pastoral staff of one of the large churches in our area. Frank, the "senior man" in the group, pastor of a historic church in the city—and Doug, his assistant. Jeff, an assistant pastor, progressive thinker, and musician. Myself.

We pick up our doughnuts, draw cups of strong coffee, and banter a bit about the Minnesota Vikings, our stewardship campaigns, the coolness of the weather. After a while, Judy, chairing for the day, calls us to order. "Before we begin," she says, "I want to ask you something. It seems like we've been hit very hard with cancer in our congregation lately. We hear two or three new cases a week. Are any of you having that experience?"

"I am." It is Frank. His voice is soft, but strong. "We found out last week that my wife has lung cancer. She is facing a series of radiation treatments, then surgery. I won't be coming to these breakfasts anymore for a while. I want to be home with her."

The group sits quiet for a minute. Slowly, slowly, tentative conversation begins again. We express our sadness, our grief. We ask our questions. Frank answers them carefully, with an incredible combination of poise, sadness, clarity, and fear. He talks of the guilt he feels for being away from home so much, and every head in the place nods. We all know exactly what he means. We promise our love, our prayers, our support. Frank expresses his gratitude for Doug, who is now taking up a big part of the load in the congregation. Judy leads us in prayer.

Now it is Doug's turn to speak. "I also have an announcement to make." Silence. "I won't be coming to these breakfasts anymore either. My wife works late on Tuesday nights, and it just get too hectic around our house in the morning when I have to leave by 7:00 A.M." There are three young children in the home. We know what he means. We all say that we will miss him, but will look forward to seeing him on other occasions.

Mark speaks. "Gee, Doug, the way you started out I thought you were going to tell us that you are leaving."

"That, too," Doug answers. He goes on to explain how a call is forthcoming from a church in another synod. He will be leaving soon. He is excited about the possibility. It seems like a good move for him. He is feeling guilty about leaving Frank at such a time, but they both know that it is the way it has to be. He tells us about where he is going, and we are happy for him.

"I also have an announcement to make," says Mark, claiming the floor. "I'm not leaving." He explains the opportunity which had been put before him, and his decision not to make a change at this time, in spite of a fair amount of pressure being put on him by the person recruiting him for the possible new post. We talk a bit about the whole question of mobility and the making of moves from one congregation to another.

It is almost 9:00 A.M., time to be finished. Judy has been kind. She has not forced the agenda, has not required of us that we retreat from our pains and hurts and dilemmas to the comfortable world of an academic discussion of scripture. As the group breaks up, we recognize our own growth and maturing as a group, that we have reached the point of such openness with each other.

By 9:05 we are in our cars, headed off for another day of pastoral busyness. We did not achieve our agenda for the morning, the study of the preaching texts. Maybe we accomplished much more.

We pastors have the responsibility to be pastors to each other. I know that is a responsibility incumbent upon every Christian, to be "a little Christ" to the neighbor. But somehow I feel a particular obligation to my sisters and brothers within the profession/calling of ordained ministry. The calling that we share binds us together. We need to be pastors to each other, pastors in the very best sense of the word.

I consider myself fortunate to be in a place where I can sit with such a group of colleagues. Geography makes that impossible for some pastors. I consider myself fortunate to be gifted with such a fine, compatible group of colleagues. That is not always the case. I hope and pray that somehow, sometime, all the pastors might have a chance for such common sharing and the "mutual consolation of the brothers and sisters."

In the meantime, partners, keep reaching out to your partners in ministry. I, for my part, will keep confessing my little craziness to you, just to let you know that you are not the only one who feels the way you feel. We are all in this together.

Pastor Luther Lutefisk Invictus

PASTOR LUTHER LUTEFISK BEGAN THE DAY WITH A COMPLEX chore. With the left-hand knob on his desk-calendar pen set pulled to the "out" position, he turned the knob counterclockwise from "Sat" to "Tue." Then, pushing the knob to its "in" position, he turned the knob until the "3" space on the calendar dial was blank. He pulled the right-hand knob out, and turned it clockwise, until the "Aug" became "Sep." Finally, he pushed the right-hand knob in and realized that it was already on the "1" and would not require adjustment. As an afterthought, he pulled the left-hand knob out again, so that, when he changed the setting the next morning he would only change the day and not the first digit of the date. Pushing the desk calendar back out to its assigned spot just past the desk pad, Pastor Lutefisk contemplated the deep existential meaning of its message: "Tue 3 Sep."

Outside the window there were children marching off for their first day of school. Pastor Lutefisk could hear their chattering and laughing as he pondered attendance and offering figures on his desk. Well, Labor Day weekend was *never* a good Sunday. Next week they would all be back, as Sunday school resumed and everyone got back to the "regular" routine. Pastor Lutefisk studied his appointment book.

"Wednesday, 6:30 P.M.–Confirmation." Another year of confirmation classes about to begin! Another group of eighth graders filled with adolescent extremes and enthusiasms appearing to wrestle with the meaning of the Christian faith according to Martin Luther–and Luther Lutefisk.

Pastor Lutefisk did not like to ask himself the question, but sometimes it simply would not be denied: He wondered if confirmation class really did make a difference in anyone's life. Were they really learning something—learning even that they had a pastor and a church who cared about them, not to mention a God to love them? Or were they just going through the motions, showing up simply because they had no choice in the matter? Twenty-five years of confirmation! Six different curricula, each of which promised to do miracles, none of which did. Confirmation, beginning again.

"*Thursday, 10:00 A.M.—Funeral.*" When first he had entered that congregation some years before, Pastor Lutefisk had taken quiet satisfaction from his conduct of funerals. All very orderly, all very moving, and all, it was said, very meaningful to the bereaved. But funerals had been proving more difficult of late. There was less of a gap than there used to be between his age and the age of the people who were dying. He had some sense of time catching up with him. Lately, for no discernable reason, he had discovered himself choking up a bit in the course of some funeral services.

"*Thursday, 7:00 P.M.—Stewardship Committee.*" The wheels were turning for this year's Every Member Response. In twenty-five years, Pastor Luther felt like he had seen every conceivable approach to stewardship. From Every Member Visits to Loyalty Sundays to Cottage Meetings to Congregational Dinners to Pony Express—he had done them all. Over the years, the congregation's stewardship had slowly improved, improved at the rate of inflation. Pastor Luther had worked hard on stewardship and had been a faithful steward himself, even when that meant a "tighter" lifestyle for the Lutefisk family. He would again speak a strong biblical word for stewardship this year; there could be no doubt of that. But on this particular September morning, the words were not exactly ready to gush forth. Another stewardship campaign did not start his juices bubbling.

"*Friday, 7:00 P.M.—Wedding Rehearsal: Saturday, 2:00 P.M.—Wedding.*" How many couples had he married over the years? Certainly the number must be in the hundreds. Earnest young couples, seemingly younger each year. Did they know what they were getting into? In a world where divorce was becoming the norm, would they find a way to keep their union together? Frankly, did they even expect to keep their union together, expect it enough to give it the work it would require?

And then, of course, "Sunday." The kids would be back again for a new year of Sunday school. Then on Monday a new week and the new year's edition of the old routine would begin in earnest.

Pastor Luther Lutefisk did not feel burned out. He sensed no particular spiritual crisis. His family life was happy. The congregation, if not prospering in the way that he and his bishop would like, was at least doing more than just "holding its own." He was the beloved pastor in the very best sense of the word, a pastor who could be counted on to radiate that happy combination of spirituality, enthusiasm, and compassion that people look for in their pastors. He was content in his congregation, and he had no desire to leave. But on this particular Tuesday morning, looking at the beginning of a new program year, he felt a little tired, a little depressed, and somewhat old.

But no one would ever know. If they were to find out, it could be unsettling. Pastor Lutefisk knew he would snap out of it. Climbing into his car to make hospital visits in the afternoon, Pastor Lutefisk made sure that all the windows were closed and no one was watching. Then, filling his lungs with as much air as he could hold, he hit the first note: "Oooooklahoma / Where the winds comes sweeping down the plain." And, by the time he had gasped his way through the letters, assuring the Sooner state that it was doing fine and was okay, Pastor Luther Lutefisk was also doing fine; Pastor Luther Lutefisk would be okay.

Veterans Day

PERHAPS SOMEWHERE THERE IS A PASTOR WHOSE DAYS ARE predictably orderly, free of the chaos that tumbles down on the rest of us ordinary mortals. I must confess that I have as many as three or four such days each year. That Monday was not one of them.

I was mentally preparing myself to perform a funeral for a stillborn. A family in the congregation had just approached me to help them deal with a sexual-abuse situation. There was another circumstance in another family having to do with physical abuse. A potential suicide. The usual dose of serious illness. A few marriages in crisis. The congregation, as is traditional, had a number of creditors breathing down its neck for money. A once-active family had announced they were leaving the congregation. The copying machine had gone belly-up. There had been no cookies at the coffee hour on Sunday morning, generating great animosity among the saints. I was half-remembering that old quote about the inmates taking over the asylum.

All of this was bubbling in my mind as I taught the Monday morning Bible class that day, trying to shed some light on the dark corners of the book of Revelation. It was still with me when my wife picked me up for lunch.

The luncheon invitation had come several weeks before from a no-longer-young pastor who had been a mentor of mine in another part of the country. He was coming into our area to preach at an anniversary service for a congregation he had served many years before. During his visit, he was hosting a luncheon for his friends at a lovely hotel nearby. Pat and I were invited, and we accepted the invitation enthusiastically. I was glad to be going, for it would be great to see this old friend and his equally charming wife. At the same time, I went carrying all of the burdens of that day.

The meal was delightful. After we had finished eating, our host got up and shared with all of us some reflections on his own recent life. Then he invited all of the rest of us to do the same.

I do not often have the experience of being the youngster in the crowd anymore, but in this case I was one of the younger persons. Our host was ordained in 1931, and most of the guests were either his peers or people slightly younger. To a person they were active church members. The majority of them were pastors, pastors' wives, or widows of pastors. In turn they stood up and reminisced about their pastorates and their old friendships.

Some had spent years serving a single congregation, building them into landmark churches in Lutheranism. Some had started new congregations in states like Idaho and Utah. Others had served in the inner city, on the staffs of church agencies, on college campuses. Their remarks were a study in oral history. I felt honored to be in the same room.

These folks did not do their pastorates in "easy times," if there are such things. They started out at the tail end of the Depression. They served through World War II. If some of their congregations benefited from the church boom of postwar years, just as many were in city churches as urban crisis came to full bloom. I am sure they all missed a few paychecks along the way, and even when the paychecks came, they were less adequate than the checks most of us now receive. They had earned that venerable title "Veterans of the Cross."

When the last report had been given, the last memory shared, the last laugh laughed, our host stood up again. He expressed his gratitude to those who had attended, and then he expressed in a few words what the others had been saying all along: "There is nothing like being a pastor and having the love and affection you have in that position. It is a privilege to be a pastor."

I headed back to the salt mine that afternoon pacified and encouraged. These men all walked the paths similar to the path I now walk. I am sure that they had bad days, and probably bad years along the way. They dealt with troubled families, financial difficulties, and rebellious congregations. But now they can look back on all of that and testify that it was good. God was in it with them. If they had to do it all over again, they would do the same thing.

It was a good afternoon. It made me aware that someday, by the grace of God, I will look back on my life as it is right now as "the good old days." By the grace of God, God's love will be communicated by my ministry. "It was good," I will then say. "God was good to us. We were richly blessed."

Those of us who are still in the pastoral trenches need the love, support, and testimonies of our elders and betters. We need to hear their tales of struggles and joys. They remind us that the ordained ministry we share is a glorious privilege, and a source of great joy.

If you fall into the Veterans-of-the-Cross category, pick out some young pastor of your acquaintance and call her up (times *do* change) and ask how things are going. You, more than most people, will be able to understand. You will be able to offer a kind of counsel and spiritual support no one else has to offer. We young whippersnappers need you.

Likewise, if you are newer to the trade, seek out one of the people I have described in your vicinity. Get to know him. You will find your life enriched, and your blood pressure lowered, by that friendship.

I am grateful to a veteran like my friend who hosted the luncheon. Such people are pastors to me as well as friends, and knowing them makes me a better and happier pastor.

From them I have gained my latest ambition. I want to be one of them someday! This young whippersnapper may yet become an elder statesman.

Moving on Fantasies

ONE OF THE GRACES OF THE "SUMMER SLUMP" THAT AFFLICTS most of our congregations is that it affords us the opportunity to sit back and ponder. That is also one of its curses.

I can remember a summer some years ago when I spent some time almost every day thumbing my way through the synodical yearbook. By August, I had progressed to the national yearbook. I would look at the statistics for this or that congregation, picture its geographic setting and try to imagine what it would be like to be the pastor of this or that church.

"St. Ralph's by the Railroad, Millville." Doesn't sound like a good part of town. Baptized members: 312. Confirmed members: 294. Must be a small Sunday school. But they didn't show any indebtedness, and they average 236 worshipers a Sunday, so the people are loyal. Might not be too bad.

"Johnson Memorial, Lost Nation." The name of the town makes me a little nervous, but being the pastor there would probably give you the chance to be a really important person in the community. I could take that.

"Holy Apostles, Statusburg." Get a load of that budget! I'll bet I wouldn't have to carry out the garbage if I were the pastor of that church. I might even be able to buy a ream of paper without worrying about how I would explain it to the church treasurer.

And so it went. Every congregation I bothered to fantasize about turned out to be "better" than where I was at the moment.

If you haven't guessed it by now, I was not happy in the congregation I was then serving. I wanted to leave.

And, while they never said it to my face in so many words, I had the definite feeling that the people of the congregation would not be at all sorry to see me go. Council meetings had grown surly. I had the sense that conversations were taking place behind my back. The faces of the diminishing number of worshipers which appeared each Sunday were not cheerful. The handwriting was on the wall. It was time to leave.

My synod president (what we called our "Peerless Leader" in those ecclesiastical days) was aware of my circumstances and was as supportive of me as the situation allowed him to be. He helped me think through what had "gone wrong" for me in that place and boosted my ego by offering me as a candidate in other congregations.

The first one sounded great. Nice-sized church in a gracious suburb in one of our favorite cities. A lovely, modern church building nestled among the pines. This congregation regularly provided leaders for the programs of the synod. It would be a positive step. Believe me, I was fired up when that call committee came to hear me preach. I had a good sermon that day, if I do say so myself.

Later in the week the synod president called me to break the news. The call committee had turned me down. They thought I looked and sounded too much like their old pastor. My heart cracked a little.

A few weeks went by. Then my name went out again. This time I made it to the interview phase. I prepared carefully. I read up on the prospective congregation. I painstakingly studied the materials they shared with me. When the day of the interview came, my wife and I drove around the community, admiring the college campus adjacent to the neat, attractive church building with its new education wing. As I sat with the call committee that night, I tried to present myself well and asked questions designed to reflect both by pastoral sensitivity and my insight into the circumstances of the congregation. As I took the requisite tour of the church building, I pictured myself preaching from the magnificent Gothic pulpit, sitting at the huge, executive-style desk, teaching in the freshly appointed classrooms, and serving these alert and committed people. I was hooked. I started to see myself as the pastor of that congregation.

The deliberations took a while. They had me back for a second interview. It was clear to me that God intended for me to be pastor of that church. Unfortunately, the Lord did not see fit to share that bit of information with the call committee. A few weeks later, I was informed that they had chosen another candidate. My heart cracked wider.

After a few days of total despair, I went back to the yearbooks, back to trying to imagine myself as the pastor of some other congregation. But, by now, self-doubt was blaring a tuba tune in my ears, and I wondered if any other congregation would ever have me.

My agony was not as long as it seemed when I was living through it. By the time the next summer rolled around, I met a call committee that decided to take a chance on me, and that resulted in a pastorate that was joyful, exciting, and fulfilling. I have never again been intensely unhappy in a congregation. When I have had the occasion to consider other calls since then, I have not been in the position of feeling as if I had to have a new call, the sooner the better.

But many of my friends have been and are in that situation, and I expect that there are a few folks reading these words who have already spent some time today fantasizing about a new call. While all of us know academically that mobility is an issue in the church, for some of us it is a painfully personal issue. You want to move, your people are ready for you to move, and the bishop is willing to help you move—but nothing is happening. You check the mail as soon as it comes, and you jump every time the telephone rings, but so far, nothing.

And so you keep on going where you are, writing sermons, teaching classes, visiting the sick, and baptizing, confirming, marrying, burying. You help committees and organizations make plans and pray that you will not be around to see the plans completed. You try to win new members for the church, even though you can't wait to get out of there yourself. All the while you are "wishing you were somewhere else, walking down some strange new street." Most pastors are professionals in the best sense of the word, carrying out their responsibilities faithfully, even when their hearts are aching and far away.

If that is where you are right now, I want you to know that you are not the only one who has ever been there, that many of your sisters and brothers know exactly what it is like to watch for the mail and listen for the phone and fantasize from the yearbook. Many have done what you are doing, lived through the pain you are experiencing, and come out on the other side of it. I am one of them. But I also know that such words sound gratuitous and empty when you are the one whose heart is breaking.

In fact, there probably isn't anything I can do to help you. But I want you to know that I have been where you are, and my heart and my prayers are with you. May your yearbook fantasies yet come true.

Measuring What's Good

O UR TEXT FOR THIS MORNING, SISTERS AND BROTHERS, IS 2 Samuel 24. At the beginning of the chapter, Yahweh is ticked off at King David. As a sign of divine displeasure, Yahweh plants in David's noggin the notion of taking a census of all the people of Israel and Judah. David, no slouch in administration, assigns the actual counting of the people to Joab and the army.

Joab is a good company man. He is not about to say "no" to the king. He does, however, have a question: "Why does my lord the king delight in this thing?" David replies that it is not the task of Joab's light brigade to wonder why, only to do and die. So the counting commences.

For the next nine months and twenty days, the army gives up chasing Jebusites and spends its time counting Israelites. Sexists to the core, they count only the men. They go through a lot of erasers, insofar as the Israelite men have the annoying habit of dying and being born, not always in equal numbers. Finally, one Monday morning, Joab marches into David's oval office and plops the report down on his desk.

David takes one look at the report and realizes he made a whopper of a mistake in even assigning the task, a thought that had occurred to Joab from the beginning. For reasons not altogether clear in 2 Samuel, the census has gone past the level of mistake to become a sin. David confesses his sin to Yahweh. Yahweh is not ready to let him off the hook easily with a mere confession of guilt, and kills off 70,000 Israelites just to teach David a lesson about census-taking.

The point of this morning's homily, sisters and brothers, has to do with Yahweh's attitude toward counting heads. Yahweh seems to be against it.

I always think of this text in January when I look off to the corner of my desk and see the parochial reports waiting to be completed. I feel like one of Joab's soldiers, assigned to count the heads in one little corner of the kingdom, bringing in a detailed report not just of how many there are, but also how many are baptized, confirmed, communing, worshiping, what their age, sex, and race are, and how many of them attended Sunday school, vacation Bible school, and catechetical classes. (Did you ever notice that these forms always ask how many students were enrolled in "catechetical instruction"? Do you have "catechetical instruction" at your church? All the churches I've served just have confirmation classes.) The home office wants to know where these people came from, and how many of them are left-handed, and if the left-handers are proportionately represented on the congregation council and in our delegation to the synod assembly. I am not completely sure why our lords delight in these things. Then, having warmed up by counting people, we get down to the serious business of counting dollars, discerning where they came from and where they went. Fill it out in triplicate, get it signed by the right people, and send it in by January 20.

Now I am a Joab kind of guy, not given to rebelling against the directions of my superiors. My statistical report is always in the mail by January 20. And, to tell the whole truth, I am a guy who loves numbers. (A few years ago, I took part in a survey on vocational guidance being conducted by a Ph.D. candidate. The verdict was that I should be an accountant.) While looking at the numbers can sometimes make a person squirm, I do not believe that numbers are insignificant. We need to look at numbers to measure the progress we are making toward our goals as congregations and as a church body. If our denomination is going to meet its worthy goals with regard to evangelism, the inclusive membership, and stewardship, we need to get a consistent reading on how we are doing in progressing toward these goals. Statistical reports do that for us.

I get a kick out of working with numbers. I recognize the significance of church statistics. Finally, I can honestly say that my own congregation has had "good numbers" for several years now. We've grown by 70 percent in the seven years I've been pastor here, and our stewardship growth has been greater than that. Filling out the statistical report gives me a good feeling!

For all of these reasons, I do not mind filling out the statistical report. Nonetheless, I reject the notion that all ministry can be quantified and measured and graphed, and that good ministry will always produce *good* numbers. I believe that we too easily pass judgment on pastors and congregations on the basis of the numbers they are producing. And, as our concern with evangelism properly grows, I see this as more and more of a problem for the church. We encourage the false notion that a *good* pastor always produces a *growing* congregation; and its converse, if a congregation is *not growing*, its pastor must by *inept.* It is our own characteristic version of the "prosperity gospel" which we reject when we hear it from the lips of others.

There are many congregations that should be growing. The congregation I serve is one of them. We are set down in the middle of a booming suburban area where growth is embarrassingly easy. If this congregation were not growing, then something would definitely be wrong.

This is not the case for all congregations. Growth comes slowly, and often not at all, for many of our urban congregations, not to mention those located in the small towns of rural America where the population is on the steady decline. Of course, there are marvelous exceptions, booming urban churches and rural churches that deserve to be celebrated. But those are the exceptions, not the rule.

Many of our sisters and brothers in ministry are grinding along in urban areas, small towns, the open countryside, and "dormant" suburbs, where growth is not impossible, but is very difficult. Many of them are doing an exemplary job in ministry, but one that does not necessarily result in spectacular statistics. If the preparation of the annual statistical report threatens self-worth, it does the church a disservice. If bishops and pastors and the laity evaluate pastors and congregations solely on the basis of statistics, then the statistical report has become a curse on the church. As David's census resulted in a pestilence upon the people of Israel, elevating our statistics to sacred standing results in a pestilence of the spirit of the people of the church, in particular, those who are its professional leaders.

Fill out your statistical reports this year, sisters and brothers. It doesn't look good in the *Yearbook* when the small print reports that you haven't sent one in since 1976. Think about your numbers, and what they have to say about you and your ministry. And then get back to work. You've got more important things to worry about than the numbers of your statistical report.

Help Me with My Corns

JOE WAS AN ACTIVE MEMBER OF A CONGREGATION I USED TO serve. He sang in the choir, took part in Lenten dramas, and worshiped faithfully. Joe was a single man in his late forties who had a wide range of interests and operated his own small business. He also happened to be blind.

One day Joe and I were walking along a downtown street when he was accosted by a well-meaning and enthusiastic young Christian (in the worst sense of the word). She charged up to Joe and started in on him. "God wants you to be healed," she proclaimed. "God wants you to have your sight. Let me pray for you, and God will restore your vision."

I was taken aback, but Joe handled the situation calmly. "I've been blind all my life," he answered. "It doesn't really bother me anymore. But I have some corns on my foot that are driving me crazy. Can you do something about my corns?" Apparently this woman's God wasn't into podiatry. She scampered away quickly.

I often feel the way Joe felt that day when I pick up one of my professional journals. Well-meaning authors are forever trying to solve what they consider to by my problems, even if those matters do not seem like problems to me.

In particular, I am tired of articles that set out to teach me how to preach. I do not claim to know all there is to know, but seminary education and twenty-two years of weekly preaching experience have taught me quite a bit about preaching. The thought of preparing and delivering a sermon does not strike dread into my heart. I take that task for granted and enjoy the time I spend working on sermons. When it comes to preaching, I think I know what I am doing, and the feedback from the members of my congregation indicates that they seem to feel the same way. I would even hazard a guess that most pastors feel relatively confident when it comes to their preaching, and a second guess that those who are less than competent in the pulpit probably aren't reading articles about preaching anyway.

So don't run up to me with articles designed to heal my homiletical blindness. Like most pastors, I have preaching down fairly well. Instead, give me some articles on the "corns" of my ministry, those gnawing little pains that can make life miserable.

For example, I would welcome down-to-earth counsel on acolytes. The article might address some vital existential questions, such as how you get acolytes to show up at the scheduled time wearing socks and with their shoes tied.

A helpful journal might also address the topic of changing light bulbs in the sanctuary. Many of our light fixtures dangle precariously forty feet over the pews. I'd like to get my hands on the throat of the architect who picked them out. These are hanging fixtures, not stable fixtures, so even one of those dandy long-handled bulb snatchers doesn't do the job. We have to persuade a house painter from the congregation to bring in his long ladders and his bravest climbers to change the bulbs, hoping that the pews won't get mangled in the process. And, of course, as soon as one bulb is replaced, another expires. There are, by the way, only sixty such fixtures in the sanctuary.

And, furthermore, if there be some clever soul who has come up with a sure fire way to keep Uncle Max from flashing his camera in everyone's face during a baptism, I herewith invite that genius to share her knowledge with the rest of us. We announce in our baptism classes that no pictures are to be taken during the baptism. We've printed the announcement in the bulletin. We've instructed our ushers to be on the alert for relatives bearing cameras. But Uncle Max still slips his camera through security and pops it out just in time to set little Mavis crying even before we splash water on her head.

How about telephone salespeople? Is there a pastor somewhere who is never harassed by those earnest peddlers of cleaning supplies, candle, paper towels, communion wafers? I've not been able to convince my council that it would be a good idea for the church to have an unpublished telephone number. Failing that, I am left to listen to sales spiels with grinding teeth and Christian charity, but I would certainly like to learn how to avoid such agonies. If you've come up with a magical solution to that problem, I'd like to hear about it.

So write to me about my corns. I need help with them. Keeping the pew rack pencils sharpened. Dealing with the wedding where the bride has three different "fathers," each of whom has his heart set on giving her away. Monitoring the joys and sorrows of the church bazaar (or, as I saw it prophetically advertised in a newsletter from a neighboring congregation, the church "bizarre"). Resolving the great debate over whether to serve Kool-Aid and cookies at the Sunday morning coffee hour. Selecting a new color for the rest rooms. Negotiating storage space in a too-small building for all of those groups who believe that they are entitled to a private closet of their very own. Figuring out where to hang another gift print of *Praying Hands*. Making good use of little Rudy's weekly drawing of the church, which he hands to you after worship each week. Getting rid of the dandelions in the church lawn. Mollifying those saints who were not happy with their family portrait in the latest church directory.

I'm like Joe. The big stuff I can handle. It's the little stuff that's driving me batty. Please help me with my corns.

When Is It Time to Move?

A S ONE WHO ESTEEMS BISHOPS APPROPRIATELY, I TRUST THAT they really do read those pink forms titled "For a Minister Under Call from a Congregation: Confidential to the Synodical Bishop," which we foot soldiers fill out each year. The form begins with lofty questions like "What significant events and developments occurred in your parish, ministry, and/or personal life during the last year?" and "What were the most pressing problems you faced last year?" The form ends with a depressing interrogation about how much one got paid (about what a single Rolling Stone earns for a single concert).

My favorite question is right there in the middle of the page: "Would you like to be considered for another call?" Since the only options given are "yes" and "no," I have stopped answering that question.

When is the right time for a pastor to move to another call? Now and then the time is clearly right. As a rule of thumb, when you make the *National Enquirer*, it is probably time to seek another call. When you return from vacation and discover all of your belongings on the parsonage lawn, it is time to seek another call. When your name is removed from the letterhead, it is time to seek another call. But the situation is usually not that clear.

The whole question of clergy mobility has become more complex over the last twenty years. Many pastors now own their own homes and find, for better or worse, and home ownership makes them think twice about moving. Many clergy spouses are now gainfully employed in good jobs outside the home and have no desire to leave those posts, even if the pastor would like to move to a new call.

One dare not be oblivious to these factors. To some extent, they are changing the face of ministry.

Back to our basic question: When is the right time for a pastor to move to another call? There are ways to answer that question from a "professional," career-oriented point of view. One can talk of chapters in the life of a congregation. Once can talk of term calls. One can talk of the necessity of making moves while one is still young enough to be marketable. I've thought about the question from all of those angles.

But they are all so vague as to leave me feeling unsatisfied. I've decided that the only real way to answer the question is from the standpoint of faith.

You see, I am pious enough to believe that God's will has something to do with my being where I am. God's will can and does work through such prosaic entities as pulpit committees and church councils.

Given the sinful state of humankind, sometimes the system gets fouled up, and the marriage between pastor and congregation turns out to be something less than made in heaven. But the factor of God's will cannot be totally left out of this equation, even when our human sin frustrates the will of God. To use the kind of anthropomorphic language that is typical of us, God has bigger things to worry about than who the pastor of St. John's-by-the-Gas-Station is going to be. But the remarkable claim of our faith, supported by the New Testament, is that God does worry about St. John's-by-the-Gas-Station and its pastor.

Therefore, I have concluded that I am where I am because God wants me to be here, and that when the time comes that God wants me somewhere else, God will find some way to get that message through to me.

Admittedly there are seasons in life during which we listen intently, hoping that God is sending out the message to move. At such times, we are in danger of confusing our own voice with the voice of God. If we fill out our reports on a day when we feel like that, we will say *yes* to the question "Would you like to be considered for another call?" And there are also times when we hope that God will leave well enough alone. Those moments also tempt us to confuse that voice. On those days, we give the question a hearty *no*.

But most days we are somewhere in between. Anxious to move? No, we are not that. Not really pursuing a new call. At the same time, if the right opportunity (whatever that means) were to present itself, perhaps we would give a listen. We cannot really say that we "would like to be considered for another call," but neither can we say that we would *refuse* "to be considered for another call." We all know cases of pastors staying too long in the same place, to the detriment of the congregation and themselves. We need to keep ourselves open to new adventures. That is why I am no longer able to answer the question on my confidential report to the bishop.

I am a person who used to worry about such things a good deal. How long should I stay where I am? Where should I go next? How long should I stay there? As if I really had something to say about it! Putting the matter back into God's hands has helped me relax about where I am and take advantage of the present moment to make maximum use of the gifts God has given me. I can affirm that God wants me *here* now but may want me somewhere else next year.

Scripture tells us that God led the people of Israel on their journey by a pillar of fire by night and a pillar of cloud by day. These pillars did not follow itineraries published in advance. Nor did they stay in one spot forever. One had to follow where they led, without any foreknowledge of where that was going to be. Openness to the unexpected appears to be inherent in a lifestyle intent on following God.

So, my bishop, my friend, that is why I left the question blank. I don't know what the answer is. Would I like to be considered for a new call? No, I wouldn't. Yes, I would. Maybe. Maybe not.

Hanging in There

ONE OF MY HEROES RETIRED RECENTLY. SOME OF YOU, I AM SURE, know him. His name is Edgar Cooper. He was ordained in 1945 and was called at that time to New Hanover Lutheran Church, just north of Pottstown, Pennsylvania. He stayed at New Hanover for forty-seven years, until he retired in late 1992. For the congregation, that was not a remarkable achievement. His predecessor had served the congregation for sixty years, from 1885 to 1945.

I knew Pastor Cooper mostly from afar. New Hanover was my wife's "family church." Her mother is buried in the church cemetery, as are a number of her mother's relatives. Whenever we would go to that area to visit "the clan," we'd hear about what was happening at New Hanover. Over time, I came to see Pastor Cooper as a quiet, solid, low-key man who put his shoulder to the wheel in that congregation in 1945 and simply left it there. Although his longevity in that call was certainly unusual, in many respects he was the typical pastor, pouring himself out for his Lord and his people and not worrying much about public recognition. There are many ways of "being" a pastor, but certainly his way is one of the noblest. May he enjoy a long and glorious retirement!

Pastor Cooper's retirement set me thinking about long pastorates. I've never really aspired to a long pastorate myself. When Pat and I were first married, we fantasized about putting a seven-year ceiling on our tenure in any congregation, and taking advantage of the national nature of our church to live in a number of different places. But I was in my last congregation nearly nine years, and, by the time you read these words, I will have been pastor of this congregation for eleven years. That's not much when you compare to forty-seven or sixty years, but it is longer than I expected to be in one place.

I've always been aware of the dangers of the long pastorate. I've seen it happen, and so have you, that a long-tenured pastor has been around so long that the congregation comes to be identified with him (I've not yet seen this with a *her*), to the extent that it becomes a "Pastor so-and-so's church," rather than "Trinity" or even "God's church." I don't think that is healthy.

It is also true that a pastor can stay in one congregation for so long that the pastor gets into a rut, nothing ever changes, and the church winds up in the same rut. The healthy tension between pastor and congregation is lost. And certainly it sometimes happens that a long-tenured pastor, upon retirement, finds it difficult to "let go" and becomes an albatross to his successor.

But lately I've been better able to see the positive side of the long pastorate. Some of the gurus of the church growth movement will be quick to tell you of the advantages of a long pastorate for the growth of a congregation. I have no reason to doubt the potential truth of that observation. However, the advantages I see deal with more than church growth, as desirable as church growth is. They are advantages for both a congregation and a pastor.

At worship on one recent Sunday, I was watching a family in the front pews during the opening hymn. The whole family was gathered because two of the brothers—we'll call them Tom and Tim—were having daughters baptized that day.

When I arrived here eleven years ago, Tom and Tim were still in high school. Their mother was fighting cancer. She held on until the oldest daughter in the family was married, but in time she lost the fight. Three years later, their father developed cancer. I was with the family in the hospital waiting room when the doctor brought his diagnosis. Their father had become a good friend of mine. We cried together. The youngest brother was in our senior confirmation class at the time. Given father's prognosis, we rescheduled the confirmation rite from September to May that year, in the hopes that he would live to see it. He did. In August, their father died.

In the two years after that, both Tim and Tom married, as did their younger sister. They started families of their own. As I looked at the family gathered, I thought of all that we had shared together in the last eleven years. The funerals of both parents. Four weddings. Five baptisms. Lots of tears. Lots of laughs. Lots of, well, *life*.

There is no doubt that the highest privilege any pastor has is that of sharing the good news of Jesus Christ. Perhaps the second highest privilege is that of sharing life with people. The longer we stay in one place, the more life we share. That is obvious. But what might be less obvious is that a long-term sharing of life can contribute to a deeper sharing of life. As I held the two infant daughters of Tom and Tim in my arms that morning, splashed the cool water on their foreheads, marked them with the cross, it meant all the more to me, and I hope, to their families, because of the long history that we have together.

No pastor should ever be identified with God. Let's say that up front. But the long-term presence of a pastor in a congregation, hanging in with people in good times and bad, can perhaps begin to symbolize or incarnate for the congregation a long-term, enduring love of God who will never let us go. And the pastor who stays in one place for an extended period of time eventually begins to experience the rich blessing of having shared life with a particular people in a particular place to the extent of having become part of that place, having roots, and having—for lack of a better word—a home. As one whose life has been more marked by change than stability, I recognize that as a potentially wonderful thing.

The foregoing is *not* intended to be even a subliminal declaration that I have now decided to spend the rest of my professional life in the place I now do ministry in. I have always tried to keep myself open to the guidance of the Holy Spirit on those matters. But, in fact, that zany Holy Spirit might be trying to get the message through to me that this is where I should stay. And that would be all right.

But I'll never make forty-seven years.

Kicking Back

STAN AND BARBARA WERE OUR BACKYARD NEIGHBORS A few houses ago. They were a middle-aged couple who represented a fusion of religious traditions, Stan being a high-church Episcopalian and Barbara a gung-ho Unitarian.

I remember an occasion when Barbara was hard at work trying to arrange a date for us to come to dinner at their home along with her Unitarian minister and his spouse. This was about April, and Barbara made it clear that the date had to be before the end of May. Gullible soul that I am, I asked why.

"Because Mr. So-and-so (the Unitarian minister) goes away for the summer."

"Goes away for the summer?"

"Yes. He goes to Maine for three months."

"Who takes care of the church and lead worship while he's gone?"

"Nobody. We just shut down for the summer. We don't have any worship services or meetings between Memorial Day and Labor Day. Sometimes he comes down to do a wedding, but that's all."

"Every year?"

"Every year."

Well, excuuuuuuuuse me!

I knew this Unitarian church. It was not a dime-store operation. It was a prestigious congregation with a lovely building in an excellent location and was rumored to have an endowment fund large enough to sustain it in a lifestyle to which most Lutheran congregations would like to get accustomed. This was almost enough to make me a disciple of Ralph Waldo Emerson and William Ellery Channing.

I never served a church that shut down completely for the summer. However—gather around, children, and you will hear the ramblings of a grizzled veteran—I do remember an era when summers were a quiet time around the churches I served, unless you were devoting most of your energy to youth ministry.

We did still worship every Sunday, although we probably cut back the number of services from two to one. We held vacation Bible school. I officiated at a wedding now and then. I visited the sick and counseled the troubled and buried the dead (I've never, ever, buried anyone who wasn't dead). But other than that, summer was a time to read and ponder and plan and prepare and get reacquainted with the family and play some golf and barbecue in the backyard and go to Little League games.

Summer was a great time to get away for continuing education. I can even remember church councils that would skip their July meetings. I am ashamed to confess it, but as I recall there would even be some summer weeks now and then when I would "work" a forty-hour-week, the way "normal" people were said to do all the time.

Change usually finds its way into our lives in a gradual, evolutionary manner. I cannot point to any one year that saw summers change for me. But I can tell you that, in my experience, summers *have* changed, and I have heard the same thing from many colleagues.

Summers are not as serene and stress-free as they used to be. The expectations people have of their churches are higher year round, which means that summer is less of a hiatus than it once was.

Indeed, summers are now a time when many congregations both keep up the programming they have going the rest of the year, and add other activities such as outdoor and weeknight services, work camps, mission trips, and special educational programs. Committees and classes still meet. Congregational meetings are still held. I haven't had a council skip a summer meeting in years.

Demands on pastors and rostered lay leaders in the summer may be less than they are during the September to May program year, but not substantially less.

This is not a bad thing. A few years ago, one of the great church gurus for pastors, Lyle Schaller, wrote the book *The Seven Day a Week Church*, advocating a style of church life summed up by the title. Its companion volume might be *The Twelve Months a Year Church*. In keeping the worship and programming of the congregation going throughout the year, without a summer break, our congregations are acting in a very positive missional way.

However, I do worry about what this means for pastors and rostered lay leaders. A study released in 1994 reported that 33 percent of ELCA parish pastors spend fifty to fifty-nine hours per week in work related to their call, and another 43.9 percent spend sixty or more hours per week in work related to their call. That's 77 percent logging more than fifty hours each week. I confess that I am almost always part of that crowd.

I have had it up to here with the old conundrum that says, "Pastors are only human," as it is hauled out to justify any and every kind of misbehavior known to the human race. It's a pretty feeble excuse. It is, however, true. We are only human, which means that now and then we have to step away from our work, give ourselves a break, and find rest and renewal.

We have to spend time, as Stephen Covey puts it in his long-time bestseller, *The Seven Habits of Highly Effective People*, "sharpening the saw." That might mean continuing education. It might mean concentrated reading. It might mean a spiritual retreat. It might mean sleeping later in the morning. It might mean getting into a new exercise routine. It might mean coaching a daughter's softball team. It might mean more time with a spouse. It might mean caring for a truly excellent garden. It might mean lying on the beach. It might mean a trip to explore family roots in Transylvania.

Whatever it means for us, you need it and I need it. We need it for ourselves, our families, and our ministries. We need to find a rhythm of work and rest, of service and renewal. Spare me that old line about "I'd rather wear out than rust out." Seems to me you're out either way. I'd rather find a rhythm that will help me remain happier and more productive when I am going, and keep me going longer.

So here it is, summer. Your church does not shut down for the summer. You couldn't take the guilt of that even if the people wanted to shut down for the summer. The demands on you are probably greater then they were a few summers ago. Being a died-in-the-wool pastor or rostered lay leader, you will extend yourself to meet those demands.

At this point I put another demand on you: Take some time off. Don't take yourself so seriously. Kick back. Relax. Let the world run without you for a while, and do not be crushed by the discovery that the world can run without you quite nicely, thank you.

I think you should find a little leisure for yourself each week throughout the year, but in particular in the summertime, when the living is supposed to be easy.

You'll be a better pastor. You'll be a better person. Maybe there isn't any difference. You do, you see, deserve a break today.

People of the Books

THERE IS A PURPLE BOOK STUCK INTO THE CURRENT READING shelf in the bookcases behind my desk. I wonder why it is there. I wonder why I have not thrown it away.

I did not order this book. It arrived in the mail unbidden, as books sometimes do. This particular book purports to contain the messages of a certain angel who's been dropping in on a guy on the East Coast for the last five years. The angel's trying to give this gent the straight scoop on how the United States can straighten itself out and get right with God.

In case you were wondering, the angel says that Jesus came "to give new rules for living." (Something about that does not sit comfortably with my theological heritage.) The angel does not like the government, modern education, taxes, lawyers, welfare mothers, or people who marry outside their class.

I picked this up in a quick perusal of the book, which persuaded me that this book was worth to me exactly what I paid for it—nothing. I'll go one step further. I found the book offensive.

But—now here's the interesting part—I did *not* throw the book away. I put it on the shelf with a number of other books I never asked for and never wanted, not to mention a few of my favorites.

I've got this thing about books. Can't stand to throw them away. I only lend books to people I trust absolutely. I've got an office filled with books, many of them older than my children, all of whom are adults. I've got books I paid 75 cents for when they were new, which should give a hint at how old they are. There are more books at home, on shelves and in boxes.

When we moved two years ago, I did get rid of some books. Sold them to a used bookstore. Got $10 for the lot of them. It was harder on me than selling our house. Rationally, I knew that I probably would not have much further use for a futurological study titled *Significant Issues for the '70s*, but emotionally it was hard to say good-bye to it. My extra copies of *The Secular City* and *The Passover Plot* went, but it wasn't easy. A few gift books containing the poetry of Helen Steiner Rice—it felt like I was pushing my helpless little children out to face the pitiless storm all by themselves. There were tears in my eyes when I walked out of that store. These are not the words of a sane man.

Now I will say in partial defense of my own sanity that I buy books carefully. I do not come home from a bookstore with a shopping bag full of books. At least not often. But $25 does not seem to me to be an exorbitant price to pay for a book, although it pains me deeply to pay more than $11.95 for a shirt, and the tie has never been made that is worth more than $5, but try to get one for that.

Books. I love them. Even the ones I don't like, if that makes any sense to you. Which is why that stupid purple book is still on my shelf.

My natural love for books fits in with something the first bishop/synod president I served under (or *with* or whatever the proper word is to express that relationship) said in his orientation speech for new pastors in the synod. O. Karl Olander was a great bear of a man, a silver-haired giant who had, to put it mildly, *presence*. When you were in the room with him, you always knew who was in charge.

"Gentlemen," he said to us, "you should not have an office in the church." (Dramatic pause, while I sat there wondering what that room with the desk and the chairs and the typewriter and the bookcases was supposed to be.) "You should have a study in the church."

The bishop was urging us to be learned and learning people—contemplative, prayerful, and reflective people—the kind of people more at home in a study than in an office. One might expect to hear something like that from a seminary professor, but this was a man who had a proven track record as an excellent parish pastor, a firm administrator, and a great "people person," one who knew how to get things done properly and on time.

He was not advocating the study as a place to escape from people, or from the struggles of daily life, or from the administrative responsibilities that go with the pastoral territory. Rather, he was urging us to keep ourselves mentally and intellectually alert and in touch with the times.

You may have noticed a few paragraphs ago that I have not completely followed his advice. I do tend to refer to the space I occupy in the church building as my "office," not my "study." It is the place where I carry out many of my professional activities, a place not reserved totally for study and writing.

Study, however, is one of the professional activities carried out there. Much of what I do as a pastor involves people, programs, preaching, paper, promotion, prayer, planning, pomp, politics, and pedagogy, activities that do not necessarily lend themselves to the peaceful isolation of a "study." I fully embrace those undertakings as necessary ingredients in the life of the pastor.

But if I get so wrapped up in people, programs, preaching, paper, promotion, prayer, planning, pomp, politics, and pedagogy that there is no time left for pondering (forgive me—I had to do it), I start to dry up. I don't have much left to give.

Not long ago I sat with a group of soon-to-be pastors

who were thinking about their first calls. They were wondering how their would-be congregations would meet their own needs for study and reflection time. In the end, that is not up to the congregation. That is up to us. No congregation is going to be interested in having a pastor who wants to spend his or her days and nights locked up in an office/study and ignoring not only the life of the congregation but also the real life that takes place among real people outside the study.

At the same time, a congregation will expect their pastor to display some signs of mental alertness. I've never met a congregation council yet that will insist that you spend a few hours a week reading. They will assume, as they have every right to assume, that you are a responsible adult, and as a responsible adult you will see to your own needs. This includes the need for study and reflection.

We, as Christians, have a hard-earned reputation as "people of the Book." That is a significant part of our identity. I think that those of us who are pastors of the church should also be "people of the books." I know that for me, books are my friends—a significant source of wisdom and inspiration and encouragement. That is why I feel comfortable surrounded by them. That is why it hurts to get rid of one.

Still, the purple book—the one about the angel's message—friends like this I don't need. Maybe, just maybe, I'll take a deep breath, stiffen my backbone, turn my head away, and toss it into the recycling bin. That should really irritate the angel.

SERMONS AND SWEAT

The Right Sermon . . .
The Wrong Time

ACCORDING TO MY DICTIONARY, TO PARBOIL SOMETHING IS, by one definition, "to subject it to intense, often uncomfortable, heat." Sounds like me, in the pulpit.

The intense and often uncomfortable heat of my pulpit does not come from a church heating system gone haywire (although, God knows, such things happen with annoying consistency). Rather, I generate the heat myself, sometimes aided and abetted by the good folks out there in the pews.

Which is not to say that I am a "fire and brimstone" preacher of the old school. I don't do fire and brimstone. At least not very often. And not very enthusiastically.

However, I do feel the heat of coming up with something worth delivering each Sunday, a sermon that will be true to the gospel and relevant to the lives of the listeners. I feel the heat of being responsible in my use of the scriptures. While I have not bought into the concept of preaching as entertainment, I do believe preaching should be interesting and that a little laughter along the way is not out of place. Those ideas kick the temperature of the pulpit up a few more degrees. When I am in the pulpit, the heat is on!

Another reason little beads of sweat pop up on my hairless pate while I am in the pulpit is that I seem to have a truly incredible gift for preaching the wrong sermon on the wrong Sunday. I liken it to the gift I have for always selecting the wrong cashier's line in the supermarket, or the wrong toll booth on the highway.

Suppose that one week the texts for the day seem to me to radiate the mission of the church. I hunker down over those texts, the commentaries, the yellow pad, and finally the word processor, and come up with a real barn-burner designed to fire up the lackadaisical with a zeal for getting out into the world and doing mission. I come to the pulpit ready to play Knute Rockne.

And who decides to show up that morning? Mrs. Illg, whose days are spent caring for a husband wasting away from Alzheimer's disease. Sam, whose thirty-year-old wife is dying of cancer. The Olsons, still trying to work their way through their son's suicide. Madelyn, learning to be a single parent but deeply uneasy because the children are spending this weekend with her ex-husband, whom she does not trust. A whole gang of people aching for a little comfort, a little encouragement, a word from the Lord to ease the pain. They are not ready for the trumpet call to mission. They need and deserve the Balm of Gilead. But today's sermon won't give it to them.

So the next Sunday I intentionally zero in on the gospel's words of comfort, and come up with a sermon that is pastoral in the classic sense. Mrs. Illg isn't there. Neither is Sam. Not the Olsons. Not Madelyn. Only those whose greatest recent tragedy has been the failure of the VCR to record *The Simpsons* on Monday night. This is the gang that really needs to get fired up about being in mission. But I am going to do nothing more than massage the self-pity that they slip into so easily without my help.

It never fails. If I plan a quiet, thoughtful, meditative sermon, hordes of children trained by Genghis Khan will be at worship, drowning out my words and destroying the concentration of the congregation with their antics. If I try to tailor a sermon that might even attract the attention of the youngsters now and then, replete with illustrations from *Sesame Street*, all of the children in the congregation will come down with strep throat, and I will be left with only the senior citizens who are not particularly into Big Bird or Cookie Monster.

The wrong sermon. I've given it many times. I will probably give it many more. But "my people" are amazingly tolerant. They keep coming back for more.

And maybe, just maybe, the wrong sermon is not as wrong as it feels to me as I stand in that pulpit feeling the dampness on the small of my back. Isaiah 55 reassures us that God's word does not return to God empty but accomplishes that which God intends.

I believe in careful sermon preparation. I cringe when I give the "wrong sermon." But it would be just like our unpredictable God to use my "wrong sermon" to achieve a great and godly thing. I could not preach if I did not believe that God was capable of getting more out of a sermon that I thought was there in the first place. Maybe Peter and Paul had the same problem.

Off Schedule with the Holy Spirit

MANY YEARS AGO I STRUCK A DEAL WITH THE HOLY SPIRIT. I call upon the Holy Spirit on weekdays during business hours for help with sermon writing. Early in the week, the Holy Spirit and I exegete the texts and the times. On Wednesday we develop an outline. On Thursday morning the Holy Spirit and I get together to begin the actual composition of the sermon. This means that I am not in a panic on Saturday night or Sunday morning. In return, the Holy Spirit can give Saturday night and early Sunday morning time to those who save their sermon writing until the last minute, the ones who rely on that old saying "I do my best work under pressure," which actually means "I work only under pressure." This arrangement has worked out well for me, and no complaints have been heard from the Holy Spirit.

When the Holy Spirit and I get together on Thursdays, the result is usually a manuscript. While I do not stand in the pulpit and read the manuscript, I am most comfortable when the manuscript is there in front of me. I've tried preaching without a manuscript, and it simply does not feel right to me. I'm not satisfied with the results. I find that I go wandering off the topic or lose my way.

So, I am an advocate of careful planning and preparation, and I preach from a manuscript. But recently I had an amazing experience. The Holy Spirit dropped in on me on Sunday morning. During the service.

I had followed my usual working pattern this week. Exegesis and reflection early in the week. Outline on Wednesday. Write on Thursday. Rewrite on Friday. Practice aloud to check language. Read over sermon on Saturday. Practice aloud again early Sunday. Reread it a few more times. The result was a solid sermon. I'm not going to say that it would have knocked the crowd on its ear, but it was not bad. I was not embarrassed. I considered myself ready.

Then worship started. I was seated in my chair behind the pulpit while the lector read the Old Testament lesson. All of a sudden the Holy Spirit grabbed me by the ears. I had certainly read this lesson during the week, but now, on Sunday morning, the Old Testament lesson spoke to me with such clarity and power that I simply *had* to preach about it.

I am not normally a person of great courage, but at that moment I knew I had to forget about the carefully crafted sermon waiting for me in the pulpit and preach about the Old Testament lesson. This gave me less than five minutes to get ready.

But I did it. I was honest and up front with the congregation. I told them that I was putting aside my manuscript, and talking to them off the top of my head. And then I commenced doing it.

Insofar as it is ever possible to say that a sermon "worked," that one worked. I could tell by the looks on their faces that the congregation was as into this as I was. I was never quite sure where the sermon would end up, but after an appropriate length of time, it did end. After the service, the remarks of the departing worshipers were enthusiastic. No doubt about it. The Holy Spirit had been at work at our church that morning.

This has not made for any major change in my own approach to preaching. The Holy Spirit and I still do the bulk of our business together on weekdays. I still write the manuscript, and wrestle with it until it is inside of me, and I am inside of it. I do not wait for the Spirit to sock me between the eyes with a full-blown sermon on Sunday morning. I have not converted to charismaticism.

However, I have relearned that old lesson that I first learned a long time ago, that the Holy Spirit is not as good at staying on schedule as I am. Now and then, the Holy Spirit does give you a sermon on Sunday morning.

The "Sermon Title Monster"

I BEGAN CREATING THE "SERMON TITLE MONSTER" FOR MYSELF over twenty years ago when I was serving a congregation that published a weekly newsletter.

Every Tuesday morning my secretary would want the sermon title for the following Sunday, so that it could be printed in the newsletter. At that point in my life, giving sermon titles seemed to make as much sense as giving names to cars. However, publishing the sermon title in the weekly newsletter was tradition, and thus nothing to be trifled with. I complied.

In the next congregation, the newsletter was a monthly proposition. One of the things members of the call committee of the church said they liked was that I had snappy sermon titles (obviously a vital attribute of anyone seeking to be faithful in ministry). I was flattered by their praise. I thought of some of the great sermon titles I had seen over the years. Perhaps if I could come up with good titles, I would be a great preacher, like the authors of those sermons.

Besides, those pulpit giants whose services were advertised in the Saturday paper always had great titles for their sermons. So I fed the Monster a bit, and came up with titles for my sermons not just a few days ahead of time, but a full month ahead of time. And, sure enough, people continued to comment on my titles.

Then came the present congregation. We're in a staff ministry here, so the preaching schedule needs to be established well ahead of time. We also try to communicate with our music professionals concerning themes for services and sermons.

Do you see where this is going? Now I pick out sermon

titles *several* months before the sermon is preached. My Monster is well fed.

Don't get the wrong idea. I do not just pick out titles at random. I read through the texts for the given Sunday, select the one that will be the sermon text, do a bit of preliminary exegesis to get some general idea of where that sermon will go, and strain to come up with a title that hints at the direction of the sermon in a seductive sort of way.

I then create a page for that sermon in my preaching notebook, writing the title, text, and date at the top of the page. In the weeks to come, as thoughts occur, I'll write down a few notes.

The process sounds good and logical enough, and much of the time it is. But sometimes the Sermon Title Monster tries to eat me. It gnaws the bones of my imagination clean, because having titled forty sermons or so a year for the past twenty years, I've pretty well used up 1,000 of the best titles I can think of.

The Sermon Title Monster also bares its fangs when I begin to prepare the sermon in a more specific way—and then wonder what in the world I had in mind when I picked out the title already published. So—they say confession is good for the soul—I try to come up with a sermon to fit the title!

One Easter, for example, we had planned out the preaching through Easter back in January. On the Easter page in my preaching notebook, I had written the title, "The Strange Case of the Disappearing Stone." But evidently I had been in a hurry on that January day when I wrote the title, because I didn't leave myself any hints as to what the title meant.

All was not lost. I did have an idea for the sermon. It just didn't happen to fit the published title. But I pushed ahead, wrote the sermon, and tried to work in some modest tie to the title. I said "The Strange Case of the Disappearing Stone" with a touch of drama, and then went about preaching the sermon I had in mind.

Only my daughter, with the bluntness of love and the critical spirit of the college student, posed the question I feared: "What did the title have to do with the sermon?"

I still believe that giving the sermon a title can be a good and helpful idea. If you choose the title before you write the sermon, it can function like a purpose statement and give some focus to your homiletical development. The title serves to form the sermon.

But if you pick out the title too far ahead of time, you can wind up creating a monster like the one that chews on my leg from time to time.

The Sermon as Sound Bite

ONCE THE APOSTLE PAUL GOT GOING, THERE WAS NO STOPPING him. Acts 20 tells of one epic Sunday evening sermon that Paul delivered in Troas. It lasted until midnight, and it stopped then only because that infamous Eutychus dozed off up in the third balcony and fell to his death, creating such a stir in the congregation that Paul had to wrap things up in a hurry and bring him back to life.

Well, Martin Luther and John Calvin were known to go on for quite a while when they were in the pulpit. Some of our American preaching ancestors got warmed up only after the first hour.

But those days are gone for good.

I was suckled on the twenty-minute sermon. That was the norm. When I was ordained back in the waning years of the Johnson administration, I planned to preach for twenty minutes. Eighteen on communion Sundays.

But in the circles I run in, the twenty-minute sermon is now a thing of the past. I have ratcheted back to fifteen, and ten on a communion Sunday. (Of course, there are more of those than there used to be.)

The motivation for this trimming is less than divine. Part of it has to do with the decreasing attention span of those folks sitting in the pews. When I go twenty, they tune out after the first fifteen, and even that may be optimistic. After all, unless you are a devotee of public television, TV gives you everything in fifteen minute bites at the most.

Another part of the motivation has to do with the circumstances and the wishes of the congregation I serve. We are on a tight Sunday morning schedule. If worship lasts more than one hour, the entire system is thrown off. If the eight o'clock service isn't over by 8:45, we'll never get the next group in place by nine. Our time frames are rigid.

In fact, even at the last service of the morning I see people leaving after sixty minutes if the service runs long. They simply get up and walk out. "I've given my hour for this week."

To make it more difficult to walk out prematurely, we try to keep worship *interesting*. That means special music and Temple Talks and assorted razzle-dazzle.

We are a young and growing congregation, so we are continuously baptizing people and receiving new members. But all these things take time . . . away from the sermon! After all, how do you keep the service within the one hour time frame? By adjusting the length of the sermon. It doesn't take a rocket scientist to figure that out. You can only trim the liturgy so much and still do it justice.

Many Sundays the sermon doesn't get fifteen minutes. Now we're back to twelve minutes (eight on communion Sundays). And on those occasional Sundays when we are baptizing and receiving new members and celebrating Holy Communion (it has happened here)—what can we say in five minutes?

Of course, a sermon does not have to be long to be powerful. In Matthew, Mark, and Luke, the sermons of Jesus are usually quite concise, although the Johannine Jesus is somewhat long-winded.

But it ain't easy. True to that old adage which has been taught in homiletics classes since time immemorial, it takes longer to prepare a good ten-minute sermon than it does to prepare a mediocre twenty-minute one.

Sometimes I yearn for the days of the twenty-minute sermon. On many Sundays there is so much great and exciting to be said that it is a pity not to have more time to say it. But that nostalgia is a waste of time. It is highly unlikely that people will start encouraging us to give longer sermons.

In a presidential election year, we hear much caterwauling by pundits about television's coverage of the campaign, which TV never gives us a full view of a candidate's positions. All we get are "sound bites," and wise campaign strategists will work hard to orchestrate those. A successful candidate will learn to say the important things briefly and clearly.

In my cynical moments, that's what preaching sometimes seems like. Preaching as Sunday morning sound bite. Better make it a good one!

Under the Lid of the Box

THE FLOCK THAT I SERVE AS SHEPHERD IS BLESSED WITH AN abundance of young lambs. More of our baptized members are under the age of three than over the age of fifty. We have a high commitment to welcoming our youngest members to worship. Therefore, the children's sermon has become a standard ingredient in our Sunday morning service.

I am not good at coming up with creative ideas, but sometimes I know a good one when I see it. I saw one for children's sermons some years ago that appealed to me, and I have used it extensively since then.

I have a Yellow Box. (Actually, two yellow boxes for two separate Sunday morning services.) Each week one of the little charmers takes the Yellow Box home. When the time for the children's sermon rolls around the following Sunday and all of the children sit with me on the chancel stairs, the Box Bearer hands over the box, having put "something" into it in the course of the week.

That "something" then becomes the topic of the children's sermon. This gives the children some ownership for what is happening, and also keeps the interest of the adults, since I never know ahead of time what's going to be in the Yellow Box.

The adults love the risk factor, dreaming of the time when the pastor will be stumped. It hasn't happened yet. Having preached out of the Yellow Box for some years now, I've learned that many children—with the urging of their parents, no doubt—can be depressingly predictable. In May and June, we'll have a run on flowers. In October and November, we specialize in leaves. Believe me, by now I have said almost everything I have to say about statues and paintings of little angels praying, about Easter eggs, and about butterflies.

But now and then something really new and different comes along. A baseball card. A stuffed skunk. A picture of grandma. A funeral bulletin. Whatever comes, it is a child sharing something important, and I trying to focus the gospel on that object.

Of course, I've had that experience common to preachers of children's sermons wherein the adults remember the children's sermons better than they remember the adult sermon. While that is certainly frustrating, I've concluded that it is because I concentrate on saying something brief and clear to the children, and the item from the Yellow Box gives it a certain tangibility. If, somehow, I can tie the gospel to a baseball card, the hearer might remember it the next time she sees a baseball card, and the youngster who brought in the baseball card will certainly see it in a new way.

So more and more I find myself thinking about the adult sermon the same way I think about the children's sermon. I think of all of the worshipers out there bringing with them their own "boxes," boxes filled with credit-card bills and pink slips and report cards and divorce papers and marriage licenses and computer printouts and blueprints and newspapers and letters from old friends and who knows what else.

They do not come to the front and sit on the steps. Most will never open their boxes to show me what is inside. But if, somehow, I can intuit what is in there by dumb luck or the guidance of the Holy Spirit (I can't always tell the difference), then maybe, just maybe, I will be able to speak a word to them that will not only register, but make a difference.

Let me run the comparison a little further into the

ground. Every now and again a mother of father will pull me aside and utter this complaint: "Why don't you ever give the box to my little Waldo? He comes up every week, but you always give the box to someone else. It makes him so sad!"

Now I can explain that my deteriorating mind is not capable of keeping perfect score of who has had the box and who has not. And little Waldo will get the box the following week. We want Waldo to feel included.

Adult preaching works the same way. I need to be alert to the contents of various boxes the worshipers bring with them, and see to it that I do not neglect speaking to their concerns. Even though the bulk of our members are married couples with young children, I still need to look at the text through the eyes of the single person, or the aging grandparent, or the childless couple. Not all the Waldos out there feeling as if they are being neglected are children.

So children's sermons are a challenge, a frustration, a joy, and an adventure—just like adult sermons. And you know, I think that preaching children's sermons has improved my adult sermons!

Doing It My Way

THE SAINTS WHO WORSHIP WITH US IN THE CONGREGATION I call home are "treated" to two different physical approaches to preaching.

My partner in ministry commits his sermon to memory and preaches it from the center aisle. I keep a manuscript in front of me and preach from the pulpit.

Since we have no clear word from the Holy Spirit as to which of these styles the Almighty would prefer, we are able to be comfortable with each other.

I admire my partner and other center aisle preachers I know. Being down in the midst of the people at sermon time has much to commend it. I know I could do it.

I keep a manuscript in front of me in the pulpit, but it is there mostly as a crutch, a parachute, something I rely on in emergencies. While I do not memorize my sermons, I usually know them pretty well by the time the sermonic moment rolls around.

But I know that I would not preach from the center aisle *well*. My problem is intensity. I get wound up in my sermons. To call me "animated" is seriously to understate the situation. When, in the past, I have preached from the center aisle, I have been a pacer, always on the move, strutting from one side of the nave to the other. Objective observers told me that this constant movement made me hard to watch and, therefore, hard to listen to. It became a distraction. So, I use the pulpit to confine my movement, to fence me in.

Even within the limits of the pulpit, I am constantly on the move. The pulpit of a church I once served had a foot switch controlling the spotlight trained on the preacher. I am not a big fan of pulpit spotlights in the first place, but this one turned out to be a particular problem because I was always stepping on the switch, turning the spotlight on and off. My sermons looked like a light show.

In my present congregation, an acolyte is usually seated right behind the pulpit. A few years ago one mother told me that her daughter was very nervous about acolyting because she was afraid that I would topple off the back of the pulpit and she would be crushed by a falling preacher.

I considered this a needless worry. I have stepped off the back of the pulpit, but I've never fallen out of the pulpit!

I am grateful, however, that this pulpit is only one step above chancel level. If I were in one of those magnificent old pulpits several feet off the ground, my well-being might be in serious jeopardy!

Nor is it just a question of where I do my preaching. Some years ago I spent a week at a preaching workshop with a marvelous homiletician who advocated developing the sermon orally, not putting it in writing at all. He did so well himself, and was so convincing in his advocacy, that I tried it myself for about a year. But even after that year, I wasn't doing it well. I wasn't comfortable with my preaching, and the feedback from the congregation suggested that my preaching was going downhill. I went back to the manuscript.

There are a variety of gifts, Saint Paul reminds us, and, I believe, a variety of ways of preaching well. The preacher's adventure is to find the way that works best for her or him.

We can learn from each other; we can learn from ways of approaching preaching that are different from our own. Perhaps we can even appropriate some elements not inherently natural to us into our preaching.

But we cannot turn ourselves into someone else, or we lose the unique gifts that are our own. Better to strive for excellence in that which is "us" than to fumble along with something "not us" in imitation of someone else.

If you are a center aisle preacher, God bless you. If you memorize your sermon, God bless you. If you develop your sermon as a strictly oral presentation, God bless you. I admire you. But as for me, I preach from the pulpit with a written manuscript in front of me.

That, for better or for worse, is me. I do it my way!

Applause Takes Many Forms

ONE OF THE PULPIT PRINCES IN OUR AREA RECENTLY GAVE A sermon on a major public issue of substantial interest to his congregation. A local newspaper reported on the sermon on the following Monday, and noted that he received "a standing ovation" at the end of the sermon.

Now there's something to think about.

I've been plugging away in the pulpit for years, and not once have I drawn a standing ovation.

It would be quite a thrill. I picture myself stepping down from the pulpit while the congregation rises to its feet in spontaneous adulation, beads of sweat popping out on my forehead as I exchange high fives with the acolytes and the liturgist and bow humbly in gratitude for the congregation's response. It is an alluring picture.

But I'm not holding my breath. Usually the best I can hope for is that most of the saints will still be awake when the sermon comes to an end.

A few will say "good sermon" as they exit–the same few every week–and that will be that. My people are not big on standing ovations, though now and then we muster a little desultory applause when the children's choir belts out a particularly memorable number with noteworthy gusto.

That is all right with me. I am a conservative old codger, so applause at worship seems somewhat out of place.

Nonetheless, deep in my heart of hearts, I think I would get a major charge out of a standing ovation. Or sitting ovation, maybe? Shucks, even the Zen sound of one hand clapping might give me a good feeling.

Until that time comes–probably the day after the Day of the Lord–I content myself with slighter things . . .

On the nation's calendar, it was Memorial Day weekend. On the church's calendar, it was Pentecost. As an advocate of good liturgical practices, my instinct was to go with Pentecost. But the Pentecost texts did nothing for me and my mind kept drifting off to Memorial Day.

Finally, on the Thursday before the Sunday in question, I decided to go with my instincts and do Memorial Day. Even though the church has its own "Memorial Day" when All Saints Day rolls around in November, it just felt as if this was what I should do.

What I did was nothing exceptional. I worked from the words in 1 Thessalonians that you "not grieve as those who have no hope." I lifted up the idea that these words do not tell us *not* to grieve, but rather not to grieve as *those who have no hope.*

It was a small congregation that day, as befits the first big holiday weekend of the summer. The sermon was gentle, "pastoral," a lifting up of the great resurrection themes of the Easter season which had just ended. I considered it an acceptable effort, but certainly no worthy of a standing ovation, and it did not get one.

But then, on Tuesday morning, one of our newest members called me. "Could I get a copy of your sermon from Sunday?" she asked. "My mother died a few years ago just before Memorial Day, and I've never quite gotten over it, but that sermon made me feel better about her death than I ever have before. It was good to hear that it is okay to grieve, and that we can have hope at the same time." I told her that I would be happy to make a copy of the sermon and send it to her.

Later in the week, a young father from the congregation stopped by the office. "My wife had a miscarriage a few weeks ago," he said. "Nobody really knew that she was pregnant, so we didn't say much to anyone. It's been hard on both of us. We've been distant with each other. After your sermon last Sunday, we went home, sat down at the lunch table, and we cried. We're better now. Thanks."

We don't usually do this kind of thing, but that week we made up about fifteen copies of that sermon and put them out for people to take the following Sunday. By the end of the morning, people were asking for more.

It wasn't a standing ovation. Most of us will never get one of those. We can dream of it, but it will never happen. Yet as I think back to that sermon, in my mind I can imagine the sound of a few hands clapping. And that is good enough.

My Three Congregations

IN THIS LITTLE CORNER OF THE GLOBAL CHURCH THAT I CALL home, we have three services every Sunday, year-round, save for Easter Sunday, when we have four.

The "8:00 A.M. crowd" is consistently the smallest, but also the most stable. Oddly enough, on a percentage basis, this early congregation is the one least affected by such outside factors as weather and time changes. We can spring ahead by one hour, we can have snow on Saturday night (not at all unusual in Minnesota), and the same folks in the same numbers will show up at the same service on Sunday.

The liturgy is somewhat simplified, but they get a full serving of the sermon for the day.

While I've been living with my sermon for several days and have gone through it from the pulpit more than once by the time that service gets rolling, this is its first public unveiling, and I am never quite sure what to expect.

Sometimes sermons that look and sound great to me fall flat when they are exposed to a real living, breathing congregation. Others that seemed not-so-good seem to gain a life of their own.

The stability (stolidity?) of the "8:00 A.M. crowd" makes them fairly unresponsive listeners, at least to the naked eye. It isn't easy to get a rise out of Minnesotans at such an early hour on a winter Sunday morning. While I learn *something* about my sermon at that service, it isn't a lot.

By the time the "8:00 A.M. crowd" is finishing off its coffee and heading for the parking lot, the masses are pouring in for the 9:00 A.M. service.

This is more likely to come close to being a full house. Representative of our congregation, it will be a lot of young families with young children. One of our choirs is usually singing.

On a good week, the sermon has had its test run, and my juices are pumping. On a bad week, I am amending and revising on the fly.

The "9:00 A.M. crowd" is a responsive group, more likely to laugh out loud at my fumbling attempts at humor, more visibly into what is going on than the "8:00 A.M. crowd."

When I critique myself at the end of the morning, I will usually think that I was at my best at 9:00 A.M. I was warmed up and had my edge.

The third service is at 10:30 A.M., and it is usually just as large as the 9:00 A.M. service. There will probably be a choir present, and the pews will come close to being "comfortably filled" on an average Sunday. Many Sundays this service will include a baptism.

Demographically, the "10:30 A.M. crowd" is about the same as the "9:00 A.M. crowd." On a regular basis, the 10:30 A.M. service will feature our "contemporary" liturgy. All in all, it is a fine service.

When I pause for prayer prior to the sermon, though, I usually pray for focus and concentration. I've hit my peak at 9:00 A.M., and by 10:30 A.M. I am starting to get tired of my own sermon. My heart goes out to our organist, who has already listened to it twice.

My mind sometimes starts to wander the third time through. I genuinely worry that this shows, for on an average Sunday, the "10:30 A.M. crowd" seems less responsive than the "9:00 A.M. crowd."

Admittedly, this is how it appears to me. However, over the years I have come to appreciate one further strange and complicating phenomenon.

I cannot honestly report that I am regularly besieged by hordes of congregants eager to discuss the sermon for the day and its implications for their lives. However, those precious few who do seek me out later in the day, later in the week or later in the month to ask their questions, express their appreciation or share their struggles are more likely to come from the "8:00 A.M. crowd" or the "10:30 A.M. crowd" than they are to come from the "9:00 A.M. crowd."

The "9:00 A.M. crowd" seems like the most responsive, and I feel as if I am at my best then. But over the long haul, as far as I can tell, those at the other two services are more "into" the sermon than the most apparently responsive.

I do not describe "my three congregations" to seek your insights as to why this pattern occurs the way it does. I simply tell you that this is the way it is with me in this place. It reminds me that there is more to this enterprise of preaching than is apparent to the naked eye.

Do you suppose that there is a "Higher Power" at work in my sermons (yours, too) than the power of my own spiritual insights and brilliant expression?

There better be.

Preaching by, and for, Human Beings

A WHILE BACK I HAD A HEART ATTACK. IT WAS DEFINITELY NOT "the big one." My little heart attack was a message to me that if I intend to be around to enjoy my retirement, and I do, the time has come to start taking better care of myself. And I am.

I was out of the pulpit for only three Sundays. On my first Sunday back, I used some of the sermon time to talk about my heart attack and recovery, to express thanks to the congregation for their kindness to us during some difficult times (my wife had been in an auto accident the day before my heart attack), and to reassure them that I was well on the road to recovery.

It was my intention to leave it at that. While I did have a few nuggets of illustrative material drawn out of heart attack\hospital\angioplasty\recovery experiences tucked away, I intended to leave them there until I could pluck them out one at a time. I did not intend to devote the next few Sundays to a sermon series built around "My Achy Breaky Heart." That would have been incredibly boring, both to the congregation and to me.

So when the next Sunday came along, I gave what I considered to be a "regular" sermon on the text, a sermon that included absolutely no references to my coronary adventures. Likewise for the next Sunday, and so forth. As far as I was concerned, I was back to normal.

Nonetheless, a few people have said to me lately, "Your preaching has changed since your heart attack." I am thinking about this.

On the one hand, I am unconvinced. Just as beauty is in the eye of the beholder, change may be in the ear of the listener. It might be that people are hearing me differently since my heart attack. I cannot imagine why that would be the case, but it might be.

On the other hand, maybe my preaching has changed.

I asked one of the people who made that comment what he meant by it, and he referred to the previous Sunday's sermon. The gospel for that day was a typical Markan text in the Epiphany season, one in which Jesus is breathlessly doing all kinds of different things, but still takes time away from the frenetic pace of his activity for prayer by himself. That was the aspect of the text I emphasized, the need to get away from busy-ness, to take time for prayer and rest, to observe a biblically shaped sabbath.

"Would you have emphasized that aspect of the text before you heart attack?" he asked.

Actually, I might have. I am a fanatic about planning ahead. I had selected the text and theme for the day before I had the heart attack. I can look back at the notes I made for the sermon prior to the heart attack and they reveal that I was indeed headed in the direction I ultimately took.

But I must confess that it is likely that the heart attack did make a difference in the way the sermon was ultimately shaped. As I lay in the hospital bed, as I sat in the chair and pondered during my recovery, one of the truths I had to confront was that my lifestyle, including my "highly-motivated" approach to my work, contributed to the heart attack.

Since then I've been working on not working so hard, if that makes any sense. I am grudgingly allowing God to run the world, and allowing the rest of the church staff and lay leaders to run the congregation more than ever before. I am granting myself more time to rest, to sit back and smell the flowers. (That is strictly a metaphorical expression. At the time of writing, it is still winter in

Minnesota, and we won't be seeing actual flowers for months!)

I do intend to make a point with all this. Whether we recognize it or not, whether we are conscious of it or not, what happens in our lives *does* have an impact on our preaching. We encounter the texts as human beings, and what is going on around us and inside of us will color the way we view and understand the texts.

That's the way it's supposed to work! Tucked away in a cobwebby corner of my mind is a quotation that says it well, albeit in antiquated and sexist language: "No man doth preach a sermon well unless he first preacheth it to himself."

As I, in my sermons, preach to the hurts and the hopes inside of me in a specific way, by God's grace the specific becomes the universal, and my preaching also speaks to the hurts and the hopes of those who gather in this place on Sunday mornings.

That does not mean that the "Achy Breaky Heart" series would have been well-advised. I still think it would have been a mistake. Our sermons must be rooted first in God's word, and only then in our own personal lives. If we are eager to preach our personal experiences, and go shopping for texts to back them up, we're headed in a dangerous direction.

It does mean that preaching is something best done by human beings, not robots. Human beings get married, have children, fight with their spouses, worry about the future, get tired and depressed, have fun, go on vacation, suffer the deaths of loved ones, and sometimes even have heart attacks. All of those experiences have an impact on the way they preach. And they should.

Yes, my preaching has changed since my heart attack. I will take that as a compliment.

Anything to Make a Point

I HAD WANTED TO DO IT FOR YEARS. I FINALLY DID. I SANG FROM the pulpit as part of my sermon. It wasn't anything big and dramatic. (I did not, as I have sometimes fantasized, wind up my stewardship sermon with "To Dream the Impossible Dream.")

It was just a few bars of "This Little Light of Mine" and two verses of "Jesus Wants Me for a Sunbeam." For most preachers, this would not be a big deal. For me, it was earth-shaking.

You see, I fall into the category of people labeled the "singing impaired." I can go along okay singing a hymn with the congregation, but left to my own devices, I'm a disaster.

What makes this even worse is that I sound great to myself. To me, I sound like I have good pitch and am in tune. As far as I am concerned, if the famous Three Tenors needed a fourth, they would only have to give me a call.

The other people who must from time to time hear me sing do not share that opinion. They describe my singing in terms that are less than complimentary. My family has a rule that forbids me from singing inside the house.

My one attempt at singing from the pulpit has had some salutary effects. Ever since I came to this congregation, our minister of music had been after me to chant the liturgy. Since the day I sang from the pulpit, he has never raised the topic again.

In addition, my singing from the pulpit has been an encouragement to congregational singing. Other people whose singing ability is not great told me that they had decided that if I could sing the hymns lustily—and I do— *they* could sing the hymns lustily as well.

Most important, at least a few folks caught on to a basic truth about my approach to preaching. As one woman put it, "Now we know for sure that you will do anything to make a point."

True. I will do anything to make a point, and often have. I once wore a clown's hat in the pulpit on Good Friday when Good Friday fell on April Fools' Day. (The joke is on you, Mr. Death.) I've worn a Minnesota Viking jacket in the pulpit. I've walked around the sanctuary carrying a painting. I had my son wheel a casket down the center aisle during Easter services one year.

And I sang from the pulpit.

I'm old-fashioned. I believe that preaching is the most important "thing" I do as a pastor of this congregation. I believe that there are two things a sermon should never be: heretical or dull. I've been well enough schooled in the system to avoid the heresy end of that. It takes serious effort on a regular basis to avoid the dull. I do not claim that I always avoid it. But, believe me, I try. I do try.

In the process, I sometimes make a fool of myself. I am sure that there were those who thought it was an insult to the gospel and the piety of the church when I wore that clown's hat on Good Friday. More than a few music lovers were no doubt appalled when I did my singing act.

I know I have embarrassed my family from time to time with my antics, and those poor innocent members of the congregation who brought Aunt Sadie to worship on a day when I did something out of the ordinary, to put it mildly, were probably humiliated when Aunt Sadie saw what a nut case the pastor was.

So it goes. I do not tell you all of this to paint myself as some kind of exemplar of courageous preaching. I am not that. I'm just another preacher, trying to get the word out, trying to capture and hold the attention of the people for a few minutes, trying to give them something to remember. Of course, eccentric behavior in the pulpit carries with it the same danger that good illustrative material does: the danger that people might remember the behavior or the material, but not the point it was trying to make. It is a risk, but I consider it a risk worth taking. If people consider me a fool, I'm sorry. I just hope they remember the point the fool was trying to make, which was, chances are, not a foolish point at all.

In most respects, I am a dull person—a vanilla ice cream, white cotton boxers, robe and slippers, oatmeal-for-breakfast kind of guy. Point me toward the pulpit, and all of my eccentricity comes bubbling out. I get a kick out of doing ridiculous things in the pulpit to capture people's attention, in the hope that somehow the gospel might hit them between the eyes in a way it never has before.

My family has required me to swear a solemn oath never to sing from the pulpit again. That was a once-in-a-lifetime experience, which was probably one too many. But I haven't given up yet. There may be more eccentricity to come.

I leave you with two words.

Tap dancing.

Journeying from the Generic

OVER BREAKFAST AND THE MORNING PAPER, I TUNE IN TO THE "wacky guys" on our local public radio station. "Wacky guys" aren't usually heard on public radio, but these two really do have some fun and cerebral laughs, and they play music you would not be likely to hear on other stations.

Those other stations are not big on such hits as "The Little Potato Song" or "Waltzing with Bears," nor do they provide regular doses of Ethel Merman, Edith Piaf, and Allen Sherman.

Another staple of "The Morning Show" is the "Generic State Song," sung by the Berrymans. It bounces along lauding the glories of the state, its natural beauties, its booming economy, its wonderful schools, its warm and talented people, with an occasional break filled by the words "your state's name here."

The song reminds me of a few funeral sermons I have in my files, sermons with little breaks in them that might say, "your loved one's name here."

I got my start in ministry in a Lutheran congregation in an eastern city that had originally served German immigrants. So, all the old German Lutherans within fifty miles thought of it as "their church," a tie that often became real only when somebody died.

We did a *lot* of funerals, often for people we didn't know at all. I remember once having three funerals in the same day. And, while I realized that it was not the ultimate in pastoral ministry, I did fall back on some generic, "your loved one's name here" funeral sermons.

Those sermons were theologically sound, even if they were impersonal. I have always had an aversion to eulogy-type funeral sermons that weep and wail and lament the tragedy of the passing of Uncle Louie, building the deceased up to a level of sainthood rarely attained by mere mortals, bearing little resemblance to the Uncle Louie who actually stumbled across the face of this earth.

My sermons centered on grace and the promise of resurrection. As I look back on them now, they were sold, respectable—and generic.

And impersonal.

At this stage in my life and ministry, I am working on holding onto theological respectability while at the same time trying to be more personal in my funeral sermons. I make more of an effort to know the deceased through the memories of the survivors, adding that to whatever I might know about them personally. While still avoiding the construction of plaster saints, I'm looking for ways the gospel illumines individual life and ways in which individual life illumines the gospel.

For example, not long ago I buried a man named Roy who died of AIDS in his mid-thirties. Roy had an incredible gift for hospitality. He worked in the hotel industry, and his family and friends told endless stories about his love for welcoming people to the hotel, helping them to feel at home, extending himself the second and third mile to make their stay pleasant, making the hotel a welcoming place. Hospitality was what Roy was all about.

In my funeral sermon I talked of Roy's gift for hospitality and of the hospitality of God now reaching out to welcome Roy into the eternal kingdom. Many of the guests at the funeral came from the hospitality industry themselves. They could relate to this. It honored Roy in an appropriate way, but also centered on God's grace. I felt good about it.

A sermon like that is harder work than my old "your loved one's name here" funeral sermons were. It is also more draining emotionally. Even though I had not known Roy well, my conversations with his family and friends drew me into their pain until some of it was my pain, too.

But while these sermons are harder and more draining, they are also more satisfying than the old ones were. I like what I'm doing now, so I continue to work at it.

I am not trying to suggest that I have found The Ultimate Answer. I am not trying to hold myself up as a model of pulpit perfection. No doubt I am miles behind some of you. I'm just telling you about one of my own journeys as a preacher and inviting you to see if my journey speaks to yours. It is a journey that is still continuing.

At this stage, I am also willing to unload my old "your loved one's name here" funeral sermons for a small price, if your taste runs to the generic. I'm not using them anymore.

While my funeral sermons were generic, the people I was burying were not.

Are Sermons Castor Oil?

MY MOTHER WAS OF THE CASTOR OIL SCHOOL. IF THERE WAS ever any question about regularity, the dreaded bottle would be hauled out of its secret hiding place, and that wretched tasting stuff would be inserted into my quivering mouth.

Sometimes the castor oil came out when there was no question about regularity, just on general principle, that twisted notion that a little castor oil never did anybody any harm.

Mom was not by nature a cruel person, but her devotion to castor oil as the elixir of life always seemed a bit demented. (You baby boomers and Generation-Xers might not be familiar with castor oil—but believe me, you would rather drink crankcase oil.)

As a youngster, I always sought to be a good little boy and a passionately regular little boy—simply to avoid the necessity for castor oil.

Now three questions that are probably three incarnations of the same question:

#1: Are sermons castor oil?

#2: Do our congregations thinks of sermons as castor oil?

#3: Do we think of our sermons as castor oil?

These questions are inspired by articles I see now and then in church newsletters wherein pastors promise their congregations that if they perform some noble act—such as raising a certain amount of money for world hunger, contributing the funds for a new church roof, building a house for Habitat for Humanity, or painting the parsonage, there will be no sermon on the following Sunday.

As if worship would be a whole lot more fun and interesting *without* a sermon, just as my young life would have been a whole lot more pleasant without those periodic doses of castor oil.

Well, I do not believe that sermons are, by nature, castor oil, although I will grant that there are a few preachers who have a gift for making them seem like castor oil. Sermons are a sharing of the good news of what God has done for us in Jesus Christ, the proclamation of grace, the declaration of hope, the promise of love, the destruction of fear, the annihilation of death. Sometimes we twist them into being something less than that, but by nature that is what they are. So the answer to question one—are sermons castor oil?—then, is simply *no.*

As to question two—do our congregations think of our sermons as castor oil?—the answer has to be *sometimes.*

Save for those of us who are in the business, the word "preaching" is not generally considered to describe a pleasant and attractive activity for most citizens of our culture. When your teenager describes your words as "a sermon," it is not a compliment. The world does not hold preaching in high esteem today.

Still, people do come, and they do listen, and lives are changed by preaching that is gospel-centered and powerful.

Furthermore, as a general rule those folks who are violently anti-preaching are probably not showing up in the pews to listen to you preach. No sane person ever volunteered to take castor oil.

Which brings us to the heart of the matter, question three—do we think of our sermons as castor oil?

I have a feeling that most preachers who volunteer to give their congregations a reward by *not* preaching do think that way. They consider what they do from the pulpit to be an imposition on their congregations, something to be endured for the sake of good health and regularity, a punishment for being sinners.

Anyone with two wits to rub together will recognize that this becomes a self-fulfilling prophecy. If we think of our sermons as castor oil, then certainly that message will get through subliminally, and our congregations will get the message, and soon they will most certainly take the castor oil view of preaching.

All of which is intended to encourage you to look upon your preaching as a wonderful and positive gift to your listeners, a gift of God passed on through you, not as a burden to be endured. Your positive view will promote the congregation's positive view, and if they and you expect wonderful things to happen when you mount the pulpit, wonderful things will happen.

So the next time you want to offer some incentive for your congregation to do something wonderful, promise them that when the goal is reached, you will deliver a sermon twice as long as usual. Then live up to that promise . . . making sure that the sermon in question is so excellent that it will be received as a reward, not a punishment.

Sermons are not castor oil. Sermons are Maine lobster, dipped in melted butter. Sermons are pepperoni pizza with extra cheese. Sermons are lemon chiffon pie. Sermons are filet mignon, still pink in the center. Sermons are the living bread which gives life.

Not castor oil. Not punishment. Life.

The Day I Really Got Their Ear

THE TEXTS FOR THAT SUNDAY WERE GREAT—THREE OF MY favorites. My schedule for the week was even such that I had time to do them justice. I did my exegetical work carefully, found the "red thread" uniting the texts, determined the central focus of the sermon, developed its connection to the everyday lives of people, and dredged up pertinent portions of "my own faith story" (to use the "in" lingo), and even tossed in some other illustrative material—and a joke. The manuscript of that sermon was a masterpiece.

Then I set out to make the manuscript my own, to get it into my head well enough that I would not have to stand in the pulpit reading to the congregation. I practiced and polished, practiced and polished.

When Sunday morning came, I was ready. As a matter of fact, I was more than ready. I was up. This was one good sermon. This would knock their socks off. To tell the truth, when worship started I could hardly wait for it to be sermon time.

Just before the pulpit hymn we have a children's sermon. Each Sunday one of the tiny saints brings me something in my "Yellow Box," and we build a message for the children around that item. Theologians might cringe at this, but the kids and their parents love the audience-participation angle.

On that particular Sunday, the young gentleman in possession of the Yellow Box marched smartly to the front with his peers and we all sat down on the chancel step. I opened the box. There was something inside. For the first time in ten years of children's sermons like this I was stumped. I had no idea what I was looking at. I turned it over in my hands, trying to figure it out. No luck. I asked the bringer of the item what it was. The cat captured his three-year-old tongue. He smiled up at me but didn't say a word. Finally there was a stage whisper from his father out in the pews. "Coral," he said. I felt vindicated. You don't see a lot of coral in Minnesota, except on the coffee tables of those who escape to warmer climates each January. However, I still had nothing to say about coral. So I talked about the circumstances. I talked about how all of us are puzzled in life some of the time. I said that we all need to ask for help sometimes, as I had asked for help in identifying the coral. I said that there is no need to feel ashamed about asking for help, whether we are talking about God's help or the help of other people in the Christian community. And then I breathed a sigh of relief, picked out another little trickster to take the Yellow Box, and announced the hymn.

Then my moment in the sun came. Let me tell you the truth. I was good. The sermon was good. It was well-delivered. But, a few minutes into it, the eyes of the congregation began to glaze over. You know the look. People are checking out the candles, the windows, the bulletin, their wristwatches, and their jaws are sagging. I tried to spark up the delivery a bit. To no avail. I was preaching well, but they were missing it. All I got out of them were a few token "nice sermon"s on the way out the door.

Eight days later (sounds biblical, doesn't it?), a man from the congregation showed up in my office early on Monday morning. "I wanted to tell you, Pastor, how much what you said last Sunday meant to me. It changed my life."

Aha! Appreciation!!! They were listening. At least that one was! I tried to be fittingly humble in expressing my gratitude for his gratitude.

"It was when you talked about asking for help," he continued. "You said that we all need help sometimes, and that we should not feel ashamed to ask for it. Well, I needed help then, but I had been too proud to ask for it. What you said made me stop and think. Then I went and got the help I needed. I want to thank you."

After he left I sat at my desk, chastened by the experience, and pondered its meaning. I thought of my regular sermon on that day as some of my best work. The children's sermon had been almost a throw-away, something I said because I didn't know what else to say. But it was the children's sermon that changed someone's life that day, not my masterpiece.

I've had that experience more than once in ministry. Something I have planned carefully falls flat, while something spontaneous soars on eagle's wings. There are those who would say that spontaneity allows for the full functioning of the Holy Spirit, and my careful hard work blocks the activity of the Spirit. That is a favorite line of those few pastors who feel that any sermon preparation prior to Saturday night or Sunday morning inhibits the Holy Spirit, as though the Spirit works only one day a week.

It is, however, too simplistic an explanation to leave me satisfied. I believe that the Holy Spirit works through my mind and through my hard work. The Holy Spirit can make use of such gifts. As often as something spontaneous has soared while the well-prepared has flopped, the opposite has been the case. Sometimes my well-prepared sermons/programs/remarks have knocked their socks off, while the spontaneous has been a dud.

The most profound conclusion I took from the incident would best be described as "you never know." It is more elegantly expressed in the famous words of John 3: "The wind blows where it wills, and you hear the sound of it, but you do not know whence it comes or whither it goes . . ."

I have learned in my ministry that I do not control the blowing of God's Holy Wind. It blows whenever and wherever it pleases. I am not really surprised anymore when it blows, nor when it does not.

I am, however, a little ticked off at the wind for not blowing more enthusiastically during my wonderful sermon.